Editors
Lorin Klistoff, M.A.
Mara Guckian

Editorial Manager
Karen J. Goldfluss, M.S. Ed.

Editor-in-Chief
Sharon Coan, M.S. Ed.

Cover Artist
Sue Fullam

Art Coordinator
Denice Adorno

Creative Director
Elayne Roberts

Imaging
James Edward Grace

Product Manager
Phil Garcia

Publisher
Mary D. Smith, M.S. Ed.

STANDARDIZED TEST PRACTICE FOR 2ND GRADE

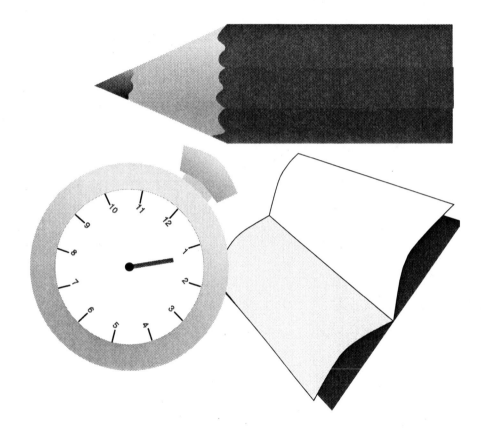

Author

Charles J. Shields

Teacher Created Resources, Inc.
6421 Industry Way
Westminster, CA 92683
www.teachercreated.com
ISBN: 978-1-57690-677-4
©*2000 Teacher Created Resources, Inc.*
Reprinted, 2008
Made in U.S.A.

Table of Contents

You have undoubtedly given plenty of tests during your years of teaching—unit tests, pop quizzes, final exams, and yes, standardized tests. As a professional educator, you know that standardized tests have taken on an importance greater than any of the others.

No one who understands children and the nature of learning would argue that a standardized test provides a measure of a child's understanding, a teacher's effectiveness, or a school's performance. It is merely a statistical snapshot of a group of children on a particular day. And there is no "generic child." Take a look at a girl named Joanna, for instance. Reluctant to speak during discussions or participate in group work, she's a whiz at taking tests and scores high on formal tests. However, Dion, in the seat beside her, is creative but impulsive. He dawdles during timed tests and sometimes fills in the wrong answer section. His score? It is no more a true indication of his ability than his doodles of motorcycle-riding monsters in the margins of his papers. You are probably thinking right now of a Joanna or a Dion in your class.

However, schools must be accountable to their communities. Moreover, issues of equity and opportunity for children require that some method of checking all students' progress as objectively as possible be administered annually or even semi-annually. As a result, at the insistence of parents, school boards, state legislatures, and national commissions, standardized tests and their results are receiving more attention than at any other time during the last 35 years.

The purpose of this book is to help you and your students get better results on standardized tests. The exercises are grade-specific and based on the most recent versions of these testing instruments:

The California Achievement Tests
The Iowa Tests of Basic Skills
The Comprehensive Tests of Basic Skills
The Stanford Achievement Tests
The Metropolitan Achievement Tests
The Texas Assessment of Academic Skills

Exercise materials designed for this book reflect skills from curricula, grade-level tests, and test taking from the California Academic Standards Commission, the New York State Testing Program for Elementary and Intermediate Grades, the Texas Essential Knowledge and Skills program, and the Board of Education for the Commonwealth of Virginia. Your students can expect to meet again, on widely used standardized tests, most of the content in this book and the style in which questions are posed.

About the Practice Tests

You will notice several things right away about the exercises.

1. The tests are arranged by curricular topics: word recognition, whole numbers, or geography, for example.

2. The exercises are short enough that you can integrate them into your teaching day. If you spend 20 minutes on test taking spread over several weeks as you approach a test date, your students will build confidence and increase their knowledge base in preparation for the actual test. Becoming familiar with testing formats and practicing sample questions is one of the most effective ways to improve scores.

3. Examples of student constructed responses to problems and questions have been included. Students must write, draw, or show their work to get credit for their answers.

The first two sections of the booklet—Practice Listening and Practice Guessing—emphasize skills young children need to know to be good test takers. The other sections are divided according to subject area—Language Arts, Mathematics, Computer/Technology, Science, and Social Studies.

Ways to Increase Students' Confidence

- Downplay the importance of how many right answers versus how many wrong answers your students give. These exercises generally have the same purpose as drills in sports—to improve players' ability through regular practice. Fill the role of coach as students learn to hit the long ball.

- Give credit for reasonable answers. Encourage students to explain why they answered as they did. Praise thoughtfulness and good guesses. Surprise them by giving partial credit because their logic is persuasive. On some state-designed tests, credit is given for "almost-right" answers.

- Promote in your classroom a positive, relaxed feeling about test taking. It might be wise, for example, to put off administering a planned practice from this booklet if your students are anxious or feeling overwhelmed about something. Use a little psychology in strengthening the association in their minds between test taking and opportunities to feel pleased about themselves.

The following pages provide a list of the basic skills embedded in the tests in this book.

Language Arts

Phonemic Awareness

Blend the phonemes of one-syllable words.

Segment the phonemes of one-syllable words.

Count the syllables in a word.

Change beginning, middle, and end sounds to produce new words.

Decoding and Word Recognition

Use phonics and structural analysis to decode multi-syllable words.

Recognize common irregularly spelled words.

Use punctuation, syntax, and sentence and story meaning to decode one- and two-syllable words.

Read and comprehend narrative and expository text.

Spelling and Writing

Plan and judge what to include in written products.

Revise to clarify meaning.

Attend to spelling, mechanics, and format in writing.

Language, Comprehension, and Response

Predict and explain what will happen next in stories.

Recall facts and details from text.

Connect information from expository selections to personal experience and knowledge.

Respond to how, why, and what-if questions about texts.

Interpret information from diagrams, charts, and maps.

Mathematics

Whole Numbers

Group tens and ones.

Compare and order numbers; identify missing numbers.

Estimate using various strategies to determine how many.

Count by rote beyond 100.

Read and write word names for numerals.

Skip count by twos, fives, and tens.

Name the nearest multiple of 10 on a number line when given a number.

Identify odd and even numbers using objects.

Divide regions/sets into halves.

Solve problems using addition and subtraction.

Use counting strategies to find sums/differences.

Tell the missing addends for addition facts.

Solve three single-digit addition problems.

Solve two-digit addition and subtraction problems.

Geometric Ideas

Identify and make figures with line symmetry.

Match congruent figures.

Recognize geometric figures in the environment.

Classification and Pattern

Compare and describe similarities and differences.

Classify by more than one attribute.

Define and continue patterns.

Identify classification and patterning in the environment.

Mathematics (cont.)

Classification and Pattern (cont.)

Continue patterns of numerical sequences.

Find and correct errors in patterns.

Order objects and events.

Metric and Customary Measurement

Estimate one inch and one centimeter.

Measure capacity to nearest cup.

Estimate number of smaller units contained in larger unit.

Weigh objects to nearest pound and kilogram.

Read Celsius and Fahrenheit thermometers.

Choose appropriate tool for measuring.

Sequence months.

Tell time to nearest half hour.

Give value of sets of coins.

Make change using coins.

Solve simple time/money questions.

Locate points on a number line.

Problem Solving

Solve spatial visualization puzzles.

Estimate reasonable solutions.

Solve simple logic problems.

Use diagrams or lists to solve problems.

Computer/Technology

Issues

Identify uses of technology in the community.

Recognize a person's rights of ownership of computer-related work.

Identify how telecommunications has changed the ways people work and play.

Knowledge and Skills

Identify essential computer terms.

Identify the function of the physical components of a computer system.

Identify word processing steps.

Interpret data on charts and graphs and make predictions.

Science

Process

Make observations based on the five senses.

Classify objects according to their properties.

Use amounts as a means of quantifying.

Estimate length, volume, mass, temperature.

Make inferences to form conclusions.

Make predictions.

Use space-time relations.

Make reasonable interpretations from data.

Identify basic properties of matter.

Identify basic concepts of weather and its cycles.

Social Studies

Citizenship

Identify attributes of good citizenship.

Describe appropriate behaviors in various environments.

Authority and Responsibility

Identify individuals who have authority.

Recognize consequences of responsible and irresponsible actions.

Religious and Cultural Traditions

Identify religious and secular symbols.

Identify symbols associated with holidays.

Identify selected famous people in history.

Why Practice Listening?

The purpose of the "Practice Listening" exercises is to introduce students to the multiple choice format of testing. Tests at this level of school are very similar to the exercises in these pages. The tests contain many choices—usually pictures—with a circle under each picture. Children at this age usually do not fill out name grids nor do they have to pace themselves against the clock. The script you read aloud is their guide to the test and how long they should spend on it.

Incidentally, it is a good idea not to overly emphasize neatness or complete erasures. Children at this age should be learning to listen, to concentrate, and to evaluate. For now, neatness is not a priority.

Answers to most test questions at this age have to do with context of the pictures. A sample question might be the following: "Which of these children are enjoying the water?"

Questions with absolute answers, such as 20 x 4 = [?], are asked more frequently on tests for children in third grade and higher.

One of the biggest listening challenges second graders face is becoming adept at integrated listening. Integrated listening on a test will require them to listen to a question containing key words such as *only*, *between*, *under*, and *unless* while simultaneously examining possibilities. This is the next step up from simple identification of the right answer.

Turn to the "Here's the Idea" exercise on the next page.

Here's the Idea

Read the script below to the children. The exercise introduces students to the practice of choosing one answer.

Teacher Script

In school, children take tests. Why? The reason is that your teacher, your parents, and the school leaders, such as the principal, all want to know more about what you are learning in school.

They can tell partly from your seatwork and partly from your work on the bulletin board. However, a test has its own, special purpose. A test will check what you know and how you think. A test gives teachers and parents clues about how to help you in school. It is important that you try your best on a test.

Look at the page with four animals. (*Check to see if students are on the correct page.*) Do you see the four pictures? What do you notice about them? (*They all have hair or tails; they are all animals.*)

Which is the only animal for riding? (*the horse*)

When you take a test, you get a book like this. Your teacher reads a question to you like I just did. You listen to the question. You decide which choice in the row is the right answer. Then you fill in the little circle next to your answer. If I put a circle on the board, who can show me what do to the circle on a test? (*Have a student fill in a chalk circle on the board.*)

That is right. You fill in the little circle near the horse.

But what if you fill in a circle and change your mind? (*You erase it.*) Let's practice erasing. Fill in the circle under another animal, not the horse. (*Pause.*) Now pretend you changed your mind. Erase the wrong one.

It is all right to change your mind. Just make sure you erase the wrong answer and fill in the one you think is right.

Let's practice taking a test. Turn the page.

Try and Discuss

Read the script below to the children. This exercise introduces students to a sample test and gives the students a chance to discuss their answers.

Teacher Script

This is what a test looks like. Pictures are in rows. The questions I will read to you are about the pictures. You choose the picture that answers my question.

Look at the row that has the number 1 beside it. Put your finger on the number 1. (*Make sure students have their finger on the correct place.*) This is the row of pictures I am going to ask a question about. Listen while I read the question. Which one flies in the wind? Fill in the circle under the picture you choose. (*Pause.*) Which circle did you fill in? (*the one under the kite*) That one was easy, wasn't it? Maybe you knew the answer right away.

Now, look at the row that has the number 2 beside it. Put your finger on the number 2. (*Make sure students have their finger on the correct place.*) This is the row I am going to ask you a question about. Listen while I read the question. Which is the slowest? (*Pause.*) Which circle did you fill in? (*the one under the turtle*) Sometimes you must compare the choices to see which one you think is right.

Look at the row that has the number 3 beside it. Put your finger on the number 3. (*Make sure students have their finger on the correct place.*) This is the row I am going to ask a question about. How much is 5 + 3? (*Pause.*) Which circle did you fill in? (*the circle under 8*) This time you knew there could be only one right answer. You did not have to compare very much, did you?

Now, put your finger on the number 4. (*Make sure students have their finger on the correct place.*) Here is the question about this row of pictures. Which animal is the fastest? (*Pause.*) Which circle did you fill in? (*the one under the horse*) But wait! These are the same pictures as before. What is the difference? (*You asked for the "fastest" this time.*) Good listening is listening carefully.

Look at the row that has the number 5 beside it. Put your finger on the number five. Listen while I ask you a question about this row. Which one grows the fastest? (*Pause.*) Which circle did you fill in? (*the one under the flower*) All of these things grow, but the last one grows the fastest. That is why you must look at all the pictures before choosing just one.

Now, put your finger on the number 6. Listen while I ask you a question. Which is the only girl with a scarf? (*Pause.*) Which circle did you fill in? (*the third one*) But there are two children with scarves. Why did you choose the third one? (*Because you said "girl with a scarf."*) You must listen to every word in a question.

Turn the page.

ANSWER KEY

1. kite   **2.** turtle   **3.** (8)   **4.** horse   **5.** flower   **6.** girl with scarf

---

1.

◯ ◯ ◯ ◯

2.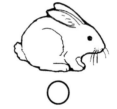

◯ ◯ ◯ ◯

3. **2** **7** **8** **9**

◯ ◯ ◯ ◯

4.

◯ ◯ ◯ ◯

5.

◯ ◯ ◯ ◯

6.

◯ ◯ ◯ ◯

Practice Test

Read the script below to the children. This exercise gives the students a chance to practice listening by completing a sample test independently.

Teacher Script

Now you are ready to take the practice test on listening. Remember to listen carefully. We will not stop to talk about each question this time. I will ask the question, and you will fill in the circle of your answer. Then I will read the next question. *(Answers appear in italics and at the bottom of the page; you can discuss answers with students at the end of the test.)*

Put your finger on the number 1. Has everyone found the number 1? *(Check to make sure students have their finger beside the correct row.)* Which person is having something to drink? *(Pause.) (the second one)*

Put your finger on the number 2. Which picture has only animals in it? *(Pause.) (the third one)*

Put your finger on the number 3. Trisha said, "I like small dogs best." Which picture shows Trisha's favorite kind? *(Pause.) (the fourth one)*

Put your finger on the number 4. Gabriel said, "I lost my baseball. Now I can't practice." Which picture shows the ball Gabriel lost? *(Pause.) (the first one)*

Put your finger on the number 5. Manny drew a circle on a piece of paper. Then he drew two more shapes. Which picture shows Manny's paper now? *(Pause.) (the second one)*

Put your finger on the number 6. Which picture shows two rows of two? *(Pause.) (the second one)*

Do you see the stop sign at the bottom of the page? That means stop.

Do not turn the page.

ANSWER KEY

1. person drinking something (second picture) **2.** animal group (third picture) **3.** smallest dog (fourth picture) **4.** baseball (first picture) **5.** paper with a circle with a triangle and square (second picture) **6.** two rows of two (second picture)

1.

○   ○   ○   ○

2.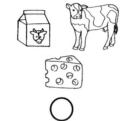

○   ○   ○   ○

3.

○   ○   ○   ○

4.

○   ○   ○   ○

5.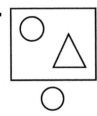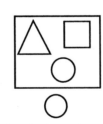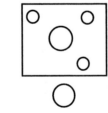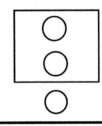

○   ○   ○   ○

6.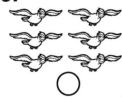

○   ○   ○   ○

Why Practice Guessing?

Sometimes students will not answer a question on a test because they do not know the answer. Faced with choices that seem similar, they opt for no answer rather than choose a wrong answer. A second reason why students will leave a question blank is because the material is unfamiliar to them. In this case, students may think they do not know enough to make a choice at all.

Learning the process of elimination teaches students to rely on *what they do know.* The key to the process is finding information in a question, or set of answers, that is meaningful to the student. Students may not know what an igloo is, for example, but they can recognize a picture of an ordinary house and a doghouse—those cannot be igloos!

The questions in this section are slightly beyond a second graders' ability level. The purpose is to confront them with a term or a concept or a set of choices that are hard to understand. Emphasize to students that standardized tests are not usually this hard. Explain that they are learning how to get rid of answers that cannot be right.

In fact, it is not important that students choose the exact right answer to each question in this section. The goal is to get them to eliminate two obviously wrong choices. Two right answers will be given for each question in the teacher's script. The better answer of the two right answers will be underlined. It is a good idea to go over the questions and answers in the tests right away to reinforce students' understanding of how the process of elimination works.

Here's the Idea

Read the script below to the children. The exercise encourages students to make good guesses at correct answers by using the process of elimination.

Teacher Script

Sometimes you have to guess on a test. You may think, "I don't know the answer to this question," or "I'm not sure of the answer." But you should always answer every question. You might have to guess. We are going to learn how to make good guesses.

Look at the page. (*Check to see that students are on the correct page.*) We are going to play a guessing game called "Which Animal Is the Most Popular at the Zoo?" This is how we play. I will think of an animal. Then I will give you clues. You will listen and cross out the animal that cannot be the one.

Put your finger on the number 1. In this row there is a turtle, a lion, a giraffe, an elephant, and an ostrich. The animal I am thinking of has four feet. Which animal cannot be the one I am thinking of? (*the ostrich*) Cross it out.

Put your finger on the number 2. Now the ostrich is gone, and there is a turtle, a lion, a giraffe, and an elephant. The animal I am thinking of has a short neck. Which animal cannot be the one I am thinking of? (*the giraffe*) Cross it out. There are three animals left.

Put your finger on the number 3. Here are the three animals that are left. The animal I am thinking of does not have a shell. Which animal cannot be the one I am thinking of? (*the turtle*) Cross it out.

Put your finger on the number 4. There are two animals left. The animal I am thinking of has fur. Which animal cannot be the one I am thinking of? (*the elephant*) Cross it out.

So which animal is the most popular at the zoo? (*the lion*)

How did you figure out the animal I was thinking of? (*listened for clues; crossed-out some animals*) The more wrong answers you can get rid of, the easier it is to guess the right answer. Remember to answer every question on a test. Sometimes you will have to guess. But first, get rid of the answers you know are not right. This will make you a good guesser.

Which Animal Is the Most Popular at the Zoo?

1.

◯   ◯   ◯   ◯   ◯

2.

◯   ◯   ◯   ◯

3.

◯   ◯   ◯

4.

◯   ◯

Try and Discuss

Read the script below to the children. This exercise introduces students to a sample test and gives the students a chance to discuss their answers.

Teacher Script

Now we have rows of four pictures again. We are going to practice getting rid of answers that cannot be right. This time the questions are hard. These questions are harder than the ones you will see on a real test, but I want you to get rid of two answers that cannot be right.

Put your finger on the number 1. An accountant is someone who works inside an office. Which one is a picture of an accountant? Look at the four pictures. Remember what you learned about guessing. Get rid of two answers that cannot be right. This time, do not cross them out. Guess which answer is right. Fill in the circle of your guess. (*Pause.*) Which one did you guess? (*doctor or _accountant_*) Why did you get rid of the other two? (*Because they show the person working outside, and an accountant or a doctor works inside.*) Remember to get rid of answers that cannot be right and then guess.

Put your finger on the number 2. This is the row I am going to ask you a question about. A whisk is very useful for making a cake. Which one is a whisk? Remember to get rid of two that cannot be right. (*Pause.*) Now guess and fill in the circle of your guess. Which one did you choose? (*the _whisk_ or the scraper*) Why did you get rid of the other two? (*Because a screwdriver and a ball are not useful for making a cake.*) You are making good guesses now.

Put your finger on the number 3. This row has four numbers in it. Listen while I say the question. (*Pause.*) Andre is seven years old. His sister Tasha is two times older than Andre. How old is Andre's sister? Get rid of two answers than cannot be right. Fill in the circle of your guess. (*Pause.*) Which number did you guess? (*12 or _14_*) Why did you get rid of the other two? (*Because 5 and 2 are less than 7 and Tasha is older than Andre.*) Good guessing works for numbers or pictures.

Put your finger on the number 4. This question is about a house. Mr. Anderson's roof has a gable that's 14 feet high. Which picture shows Mr. Anderson's gable? (*Pause.*) Guess and fill in the circle. Which one did you guess? (*the chimney or _the gable_*) Why did you get rid of the other two? (*Because you couldn't see a roof at all.*)

Put your finger on the number 5. This is the last question. It is about shapes. Which picture shows a right triangle? (*Pause.*) Get rid of two. Make your guess and fill in the circle. (*Pause.*) Which one did you choose? (*the scalene or _right triangle_*) Why didn't you choose the other two? (*Because they are not triangles.*) Learning to be a good guesser is learning to get rid of answers that cannot be right.

ANSWER KEY

1. accountant (third picture) **2.** whisk (fourth picture) **3.** (14) **4.** the gable (first picture)
5. right triangle (fourth picture)

1.

○ ○ ○ ○

2.

○ ○ ○ ○

3.

14   12   5   2

○ ○ ○ ○

4.

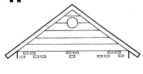  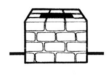 

○ ○ ○ ○

5.

 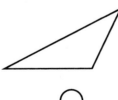 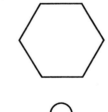 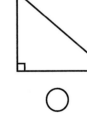

○ ○ ○ ○

Practice Test

Read the script below to the children. This sample test will help children practice guessing independently.

Teacher Script

Now that we have done some questions together and talked about them, it is time for you to try some on your own. I will ask a question about the pictures in each row. You will get rid of two answers. Then you will make a good guess, and fill in the circle under it. We will not talk about your guesses until the end. You must listen quietly to the question.

Put your finger on the number 1. This is the row of pictures I am going to ask you a question about. Listen to the question. A long time ago, people wrote with a quill pen. Which picture shows a quill pen? *(Pause.) (the fourth picture)* Mark your answer.

Put your finger on the number 2. Here is the next question. Jessica said, "Look! That fish sees its reflection in the mirror." Which picture shows a fish looking at its reflection? *(Pause.) (the second picture)* Make a good guess.

Put your finger on the number 3. Here is the question. Mr. Webb's umbrella protected him from the inclement weather. Which picture shows Mr. Webb protected by his umbrella from inclement weather? *(Pause.) (the third picture)*

Put your finger on the number 4. Here is the question. Mother said, "When you set the table, please make the plates and silverware symmetrical. That looks neater." Which picture shows the table set the way Mother wants it? *(Pause.) (the second picture)*

Put your finger on the number 5. Here is the question. Crustaceans are a kind of sea animals whose bodies are covered by a hard shell. Which picture shows a crustacean? *(Pause.) (the third picture)*

Put your finger on the number 6. Here is the question. Which picture shows three parallel lines? *(Pause.) (the second picture)*

Do you see the stop sign at the bottom of the page? That means stop. Do not turn the page.

ANSWER KEY

1. quill pen (fourth picture) **2.** fish looking at a mirror (second picture) **3.** man with open umbrella in rainy weather (third picture) **4.** table with symmetrical setting (second picture) **5.** lobster (third picture) **6.** three parallel lines (second picture)

Practice Guessing *(cont.)*

1.

○   ○   ○   ○

2.

○   ○   ○   ○

3.

○   ○   ○   ○

4.

○   ○   ○   ○

5.

○   ○   ○   ○

6.

○   ○   ○   ○

STOP

Language Arts: Phonemic Awareness

Phonemic awareness is the awareness of speech sounds. In second grade, phonemic skills include the following:

- blending the phonemes of one-syllable words.

- segmenting the phonemes of one-syllable words.

- counting the syllables in a word.

- changing beginning, middle, and end sounds to produce new words.

Teacher Script

Now it is time to practice choosing the right sounds of letters and of words. I will ask you questions about each row. You must listen carefully. I will not stop to discuss the answers, but I will go slowly enough for you. Remember to make good guesses like we have been practicing.

Put your finger on the number 1. Here is the question. Which picture begins with the same sound as "clock"? (*Pause.*) (*clown*)

Put your finger on the number 2. Here is the question. Which picture is the word I am sounding out: "d...o...g"? (*Pause.*) (*dog*)

Put your finger on the number 3. You must listen carefully. Which picture rhymes with "dig"? (*Pause.*) (*pig*)

Put your finger on the number 4. Which picture is the word I am sounding out: "b...a...t"? (*Pause.*) (*bat*)

Put your finger on the number 5. Listen carefully. Which word begins with the "sh" sound like in "show"? (*Pause.*) (*shoe*)

Put your finger on the number 6. This is the row we are on now. Here is the question. Which word rhymes with "sat." (*Pause.*) (*mat*)

Turn the page.

1.

2.

3.

4.

5.

| snowman | shoe | star | fish |

6.

| milk | man | mat | sun |

Teacher Script *(cont.)*

Put your finger on the number 7. This is the row I am going to ask a question about now. Which picture begins with the same sound as "train"? *(Pause.)* *(truck)*

Put your finger on the number 8. Here is the question. Which word ends with the same sound as "hope"? *(Pause.)* *(rope)*

Put your finger on the number 9. Which picture rhymes with "house"? *(Pause.)* *(mouse)*

Put your finger on the number 10. This is a question about syllables or how many sound parts a word has. How many syllables are there in the word "table"? Fill in the circle under the number of your guess. The word is "table." *(Pause.)* *(2)*

Put your finger on the number 11. How many syllables or sound parts are there in the word "mother?" Fill in the circle under the number of your guess. The word is "mother." *(Pause.)* *(2)*

Put your finger on the number 12. Which word in the row has one syllable? *(Pause.)* *(house)*

Turn the page.

7.

◯   ◯   ◯   ◯

8.

hop	sat	rope	roll
◯	◯	◯	◯

9.

◯   ◯   ◯   ◯

10.

1	2	3	4
◯	◯	◯	◯

11.

1	2	3	4
◯	◯	◯	◯

12.

chicken	turtle	umbrella	house
◯	◯	◯	◯

Teacher Script *(cont.)*

Put your finger on the number 13. This is the row I am going to ask a question about. Which word has two syllables? *(Pause.)* *(lion)*

Put your finger on the number 14. *(Pause.)* If we change the "p" in "pig" to an "r," now which word is it? *(Pause.)* *(rig)*

Put your finger on the number 15. You must listen. *(Pause.)* If we change the "a" in "hat" to an "o," which word is it now? *(Pause.)* *(hot)*

Put your finger on the number 16. If we change the "m" in "make" to a "t" which word is it now? *(Pause.)* *(take)*

Put your finger on the number 17. If we change the "t" in "plate" to an "n," which word is it now? *(Pause.)* *(plane)*

Put your finger on the number 18. If we say "wheat" without the "wh" sound, which word is it now? *(Pause.)* *(eat)*

Now we stop.

ANSWER KEY

1. clown **2.** dog **3.** pig **4.** bat **5.** shoe **6.** mat **7.** truck **8.** rope **9.** mouse **10.** (2)
11. (2) **12.** house **13.** lion **14.** rig **15.** hot **16.** take **17.** plane **18.** eat

---

13.

bear	kite	ring	lion
○	○	○	○

14.

fig	dig	rig	rug
○	○	○	○

15.

hot	hit	hut	home
○	○	○	○

16.

cake	take	turn	snake
○	○	○	○

17.

plant	plot	plane	nut
○	○	○	○

18.

at	eat	feet	it
○	○	○	○

STOP

Language Arts: Decoding and Word Recognition

This language arts section includes the following:

- using phonics and structural analysis to decode multi-syllable words.
- recognizing common irregularly spelled words.
- using punctuation, syntax, and sentence and story meaning to decode one- and two-syllable words.
- reading and comprehending narrative and expository text.

Teacher Script

In this part of the test, you will answer questions about words. There is a sample at the top of your page. Sound out the word silently to yourself. Choose the picture that goes with the word.

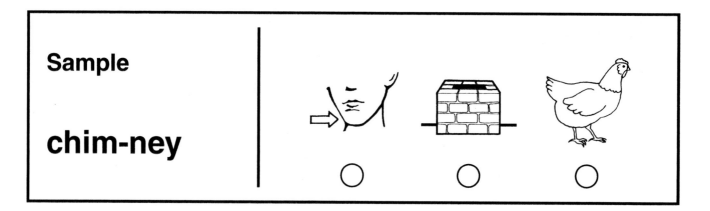

Sample

chim-ney

The word is chimney, isn't it? So you would fill in the circle beside the picture of the chimney. Now let's read the first word.

You should be looking at number 1. Here is the word. Sound out the word silently to yourself. Choose the picture that goes with the word. (*Pause.*) (*third picture*)

Now look at number 2. Here is the next word. Sound out the word for yourself. Choose the picture that goes with the word. (*Pause.*) (*second picture*)

Now see number 3. Sound it out for yourself. Choose the picture that goes with the word. (*Pause.*) (*third picture*)

Go to number 4. Here is the fourth word. Sound out the word for yourself. Choose the picture that goes with the word. (*Pause.*) (*second picture*)

Look at the number 5. Sound out the word for yourself. Choose the picture that goes with the word. (*Pause.*) (*third picture*)

The number 6 is the last one on this page. Sound out the word for yourself. Choose the picture that goes with the word. (*Pause.*) (*third picture*)

Now stop.

ANSWER KEY

1. foot-ball (third picture) **2.** door-bell (second picture) **3.** tick-et (third picture) **4.** fire-man (second picture) **5.** par-ty (third picture) **6.** book-case (third picture)

Sample

chim-ney

○   ○   ○

1.

foot-ball

○   ○   ○

2.

door-bell

○   ○   ○

3.

tick-et

○   ○   ○

4.

fire-man

○   ○   ○

5.

par-ty

○   ○   ○

6.

book-case

○   ○   ○

Teacher Script

In this part of the test, you will see three words. One of them does not rhyme with the other two. You fill in the circle of the word that does not rhyme. Here is a sample. Read the three words silently. Fill in the circle of the word that does not rhyme with the other two.

Sample

ate   great   taste

○   ○   ○

Which word did you choose? Was it "taste"? Why? (*discussion*) Now you will read each row of three words on your own. Choose the word that does not rhyme. Stop when you see the stop sign at the bottom of the page.

ANSWER KEY

1. sad

2. eat

3. way

4. ear

5. take

6. my

7. mommy

8. place

Sample

ate	great	taste
○	○	○

1.

said	head	sad
○	○	○

2.

eye	eat	pie
○	○	○

3.

nail	way	pale
○	○	○

4.

fair	bear	ear
○	○	○

5.

cheek	take	sneak
○	○	○

6.

my	weigh	stay
○	○	○

7.

money	mommy	funny
○	○	○

8.

sneeze	please	place
○	○	○

STOP

Language Arts: Decoding and Word Recognition *(cont.)*

Teacher Script

In this part of the test, you will read a story, but sometimes a word is missing. You will choose which word is missing. Here is a sample. I will read the sentence aloud. Then you fill in the circle next to the word that is missing. *(Read the sentence.)* Now, you choose which word is missing. *(Pause.)*

Sample

Mr. Miller had a store. In his _____ he had things to buy.

house	**store**	**room**
○	○	○

Which word did you choose? The answer is store. Look for the clues. The first sentence says he has a store. The second sentence says he has things to buy. *(Discuss why "house" and "room" are not the best guesses.)*

Now you will read the story silently to yourself. *(If the story seems too difficult, read it aloud. Students can follow along and choose their answers.)* Then choose the word that is missing. Stop when you see the stop sign at the bottom of the page.

ANSWER KEY

sad

picture

find

idea

place

home

dinner

rang

went

dirty

thank

Sample

Mr. Miller had a store. In his _____ he had things to buy.

○ house   ○ store   ○ room

The Cat Who Ran Away

I had a cat. Its name was Dot. It was white and black.

One day Dot ran away. I was so _____. My mother said, "I have an

○ happy   ○ sad   ○ cry

idea. We will put a _____ in the store. We will say, "Dot is lost.

○ name   ○ cat   ○ picture

Please _____ Dot for us." I said, "Good _____!"

○ feed   ○ like   ○ find   ○ dog   ○ day   ○ idea

So we went to the store. There was a _____ for pictures. We did

○ place   ○ name   ○ light

what mother said. Then we went _____.

○ car   ○ home   ○ other

That night, we had _____. The phone _____. My

○ dinner   ○ sleep   ○ show   ○ call   ○ rang   ○ stop

mother talked to a lady on the phone. "She has found Dot!" my mother said.

We _____ to the lady's house. Dot was wet and _____.

○ on   ○ went   ○ are   ○ dirty   ○ no   ○ sleep

Dot said, "Meow! Meow!" We said _____ you to the lady. We went

○ yes   ○ take   ○ thank

home. Now Dot is with us again.

STOP

Language Arts: Spelling and Writing

This section covers spelling and writing skills that are very important in the second grade including the following:

- planning and judging about what to include in written products.
- revising to clarify meaning.
- attending to spelling, mechanics, and format in writing.

Teacher Script

In this part of the test, you will answer questions about writing. I will ask you questions, and you will fill in the circle of your answer. Here is a sample. Listen to my question. You are writing about pets. Which idea does not belong when you are writing about pets? (*Read the words aloud.*) Fill in the circle of your answer. (*Pause.*)

Sample

food	**water**	**bike**	**cage**
○	○	○	○

Which idea does not belong? Did you fill in "food"? No, all pets need food. Did you fill in "water"? No, all pets need water. Did you fill in "cage"? No, many pets live in a cage. But what about "bike"? Bike is an idea that does not belong with pets. So that is the answer you should have chosen.

Go to number 1. Here is my question. You are writing about going swimming. Which idea does not belong with swimming? (*Read the words aloud.*) Fill in the circle of your answer. (*snow*)

Go to number 2. Now, you are writing about a birthday party. Which idea does not belong with birthday party? (*Read the words aloud.*) Fill in the circle of your answer. (*car*)

Go to number 3. Now, you are writing about farm animals. Which idea does not belong with farm animals? (*Read the words aloud.*) Fill in the circle of your answer. (*doll*)

Go to number 4. You are writing about trains. Which idea does not belong with trains? (*Read the words aloud.*) Fill in the circle of your answer. (*shirt*)

Go to number 5. You are writing about sleep. Which idea does not belong with sleep? (*Read the words aloud.*) Fill in the circle of your answer. (*soap*)

The last one is number 6. Go to number 6. You are writing about school. Which idea does not belong with school? (*Read the words aloud.*) Fill in the circle of your answer. (*stone*)

Now stop.

ANSWER KEY

1. snow **2.** car **3.** doll **4.** shirt **5.** soap **6.** stone

---

Sample

food	water	bike	cage
○	○	○	○

1.

waves	snow	sand	shells
○	○	○	○

2.

candles	cake	games	car
○	○	○	○

3.

eggs	doll	barn	hay
○	○	○	○

4.

whistle	tracks	engine	shirt
○	○	○	○

5.

soap	night	pillow	dream
○	○	○	○

6.

paper	desk	recess	stone
○	○	○	○

Teacher Script

In this part of the test, there is something wrong with the sentences. Either the wrong word is used, or the punctuation is wrong. Here are two samples. Read the first sentence silently. Look at the word that is bold.

Sample 1	○ Him
	○ Them
Us had soup today.	○ We

The bold word is "us," but that is not the right word for the sentence. Fill in the circle next to the word that is right. (*Pause.*) Did you choose "We"? Yes, "we" is the right word for the sentence. It is not "Us had soup today." The correct sentence is "We had soup today."

Now look at the second sample. Read it silently to yourself. Look at the spot that is underlined.

Sample 2	○ !
	○ ?
"Run __ We are late."	○ ,

There is a punctuation mark missing here. Fill in the circle next to the punctuation that belongs after the word "Run." (*Pause.*) Did you fill in the circle for the exclamation mark? (*Write an exclamation mark on the board.*) Yes, you need an exclamation point there—"Run! We are late."

Now do the eight sentences on your own. Read them. Fill in the circle next to your answer. Stop when you see the stop sign at the bottom of the page.

ANSWER KEY

1. she
2. does
3. ran
4. bites
5. ?
6. ,
7. !
8. .

Sample 1

Us had soup today.

- ○ Him
- ○ Them
- ○ We

Sample 2

Run_ We are late.

- ○ !
- ○ ?
- ○ ,

1.

Why is **her** crying?

- ○ they
- ○ she
- ○ him

2.

What **do** it say?

- ○ does
- ○ am
- ○ is

3.

He **run** away.

- ○ rans
- ○ ran
- ○ running

4.

My dog **bite**.

- ○ biting
- ○ bitten
- ○ bites

5.

Do you like it _

- ○ !
- ○ ,
- ○ ?

6.

Hey_ where is he?

- ○ !
- ○ ,
- ○ ?

7.

Look_ There's a horse.

- ○ !
- ○ .
- ○ ?

8.

Please say thank you_

- ○ .
- ○ ,
- ○ ?

STOP

Language Arts: Language, Comprehension, and Response

This section covers second grade language skills including:

- predicting and explaining what will happen next in stories.
- recalling facts and details from text.
- connecting information from expository selections to personal experience and knowledge.
- responding to how, why, and what-if questions about texts.
- interpreting information from diagrams, charts, and maps.

Teacher Script

Look at the page. Are you on the right page? (*Check to make sure students are on the correct page.*) Now I am going to read you a story. It is about someone named Arlo. Arlo orders gardening tools by mail. How does it work when you order something by mail? (*discussion*) Have you ever sent away for something by mail? (*discussion*) Do you expect to get what you ordered? (*discussion*) What if you get the wrong thing sent to you? (*discussion*) You'll see what Arlo did.

I will stop during the story and ask you a question. We will not talk about the answer. You will fill in the circle of your answer. Listen carefully to the story and the questions I will ask. (*Begin the story, stopping at the breaks to ask students the question.*)

Arlo Orders By Mail

Arlo lived in a house with trees. The air was turning cold.

"Summer is over," he said. "The leaves will be falling soon."

When he got his mail the next day, there was a postcard.

It said, "Get ready for fall! Order a shovel and rake now."

"Shovel and rake?" said Arlo. "Great, I need a shovel and rake for fall."

So he called the phone number on the card and ordered a shovel and rake.

The next day, he got a box in the mail.

It said, "To Arlo: cups and plates."

"Cups and plates? I ordered a shovel and rake."

He called the phone number on the card and said,

"Please send me a shovel and rake, not cups and plates."

Put your finger on the number 1. This is the row for the question I am going to ask. Here it is. What did Arlo order by mail? Fill in the circle of your answer. (*Pause.*) (*shovel and rake*) Now here is more of the story.

The next day, the box of cups and plates was gone.
There was a new box outside Arlo's door.

Teacher Script *(cont.)*

He opened it.

"Who are you?" Arlo said.

"Friendly snake."

"Friendly snake? I ordered a shovel and rake."

"Shovel and rake?" said the snake. "Not cups and plates?"

"No."

"Not a friendly snake?"

"No."

"Sorry, our mistake."

Arlo called the phone number. "No friendly snake, no cups and plates, just a shovel and snake—I mean, a shovel and rake! That's all. And hurry, the leaves are turning gold."

Put your finger on the number 2. Here is the question. What time of year is it in the story? Fill in the circle of your answer. *(Pause.)* *(leaves falling)* Now, here is more of the story.

The next day the box with the friendly snake was gone.

There was a new box.

It said, "To Arlo: Instant lake. Just add water."

"Instant lake? Instant lake?" said Arlo. "This isn't what I ordered. I ordered a shovel and rake."

Put your finger on the number 3. Here is the question. What do you think Arlo will do next? Fill in the circle of your answer. *(Pause.)* *(man telephoning)*

He called the phone number. "No instant lake, cups and plates, or a friendly snake. I need a shovel and rake!"

The next day, the box of instant lake was gone.

There was a new box.

It said, "To Arlo: Mix-and-bake chocolate cake."

Teacher Script *(cont.)*

"I can't wait," Arlo said. "I can't wait any longer for a shovel and rake. It's getting too late. The leaves are falling."

He called the phone number. "You have sent me cups and plates, a friendly snake, an instant lake, and a mix-and-bake chocolate cake. I need a shovel and rake!"

"Airplane brake?"

"No, shovel and rake."

"Dates in a crate?"

"No, no!"

Put your finger on the number 4. What is another word that would rhyme with "brake" and "rake"? Fill in the circle of your answer. *(Pause.)* *(shake)*

"Spell what you want, please," said the person on the phone to Arlo.
Arlo spelled what he wanted. "S-H-O-V-E-L A-N-D R-A-K-E."

"Got it, great."

"And hurry," said Arlo. "It's getting so late."

The next day, the box of mix-and-bake chocolate cake was gone.

There was a new box.

Put your finger on the number 5. What do you think will be in the box this time? Fill in the circle of your answer. *(Pause.)* *(shovel and rake)*

The new box said, "To Arlo: Shovel and rake. Sorry, our mistake."

Arlo took out the shovel and rake. They were just what he needed.

He raked the leaves. He used the shovel in his garden.

Then he jumped in a great big pile of leaves.

"A shovel and rake, just what I needed, and not too late," he said.

The End.

Put your finger on the number 6. Here is the question. How did Arlo get what he wanted at last? Fill in the circle of your answer. *(Pause.)* *(He spelled it.)*

Now stop.

ANSWER KEY

1. shovel and rake **2.** leaves falling **3.** man telephoning **4.** shake **5.** shovel and rake **6.** He spelled it.

Language Arts: Language, Comprehension, and Response *(cont.)*

1. ○   ○   ○   ○

2. ○   ○   ○   ○

3. ○   ○   ○   ○

4. **rain**   **shake**   **wood**   **stamp**

    ○   ○   ○   ○

5. ○   ○   ○   ○

6. **He cried.**   **He did nothing.**   **He went home.**   **He spelled it.**

    ○   ○   ○   ○

Language Arts: Language, Comprehension, and Response (cont.)

Teacher Script

In this part of the test, you will answer questions about a picture you see. These pictures show information. You look at the picture or map, and fill in the circle next to the answer you choose. Here is a sample.

Sample

Heidi	(crayons)	○ Heidi
Lauren	(crayons)	○ Lauren
Kyle	(crayons)	○ Kyle
Andrew	(crayons)	○ Andrew

Look at this chart. It is about how many crayons each child has: Heidi, Lauren, Kyle, and Andrew. Here is my question: Who has the most crayons? Fill in the circle next to your answer. (*Pause.*) Which child has the most crayons? Lauren does.

Now you will look at the pictures or maps and answer the question when I read it to you.

Go to number 1. Here are four pies. The name of the child who ate the pie is below each pie. Who ate the most pie? (*Pause.*) (*Tiffany*)

Now go to number 2. Here are four children standing in a row. Their names are underneath. Who is the tallest? (*Pause.*) (*Carson*)

Now go to question number 3. Look at the map. Who lives nearest the park? (*Pause.*) (*Spencer*)

Now go to question number 4. Look at the map of the state of Illinois with four cities. Which city is farthest from Lake Michigan? (*Pause.*) (*Carbondale*)

Now stop.

ANSWER KEY

1. Tiffany **2.** Carson **3.** Spencer **4.** Carbondale

Language Arts: Language, Comprehension, and Response (cont.)

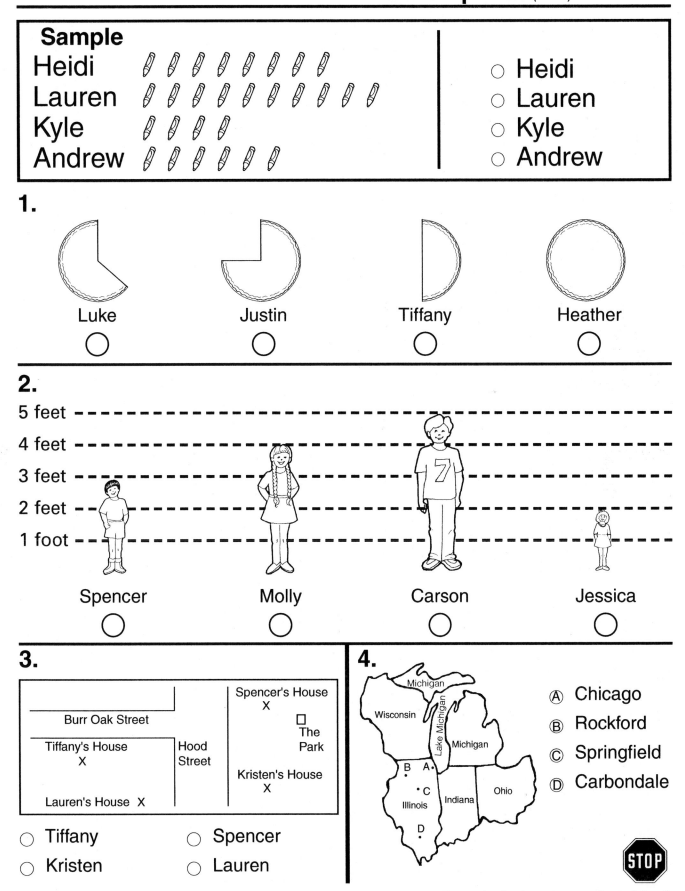

Sample

Heidi	✎ ✎ ✎ ✎ ✎ ✎ ✎	○ Heidi
Lauren	✎ ✎ ✎ ✎ ✎ ✎ ✎ ✎ ✎	○ Lauren
Kyle	✎ ✎ ✎ ✎	○ Kyle
Andrew	✎ ✎ ✎ ✎ ✎ ✎	○ Andrew

1.

Luke ○   Justin ○   Tiffany ○   Heather ○

2.

5 feet
4 feet
3 feet
2 feet
1 foot

Spencer ○   Molly ○   Carson ○   Jessica ○

3.

Burr Oak Street
Tiffany's House X
Laurens's House X
Hood Street
Spencer's House X
☐ The Park
Kristen's House X

○ Tiffany   ○ Spencer
○ Kristen   ○ Lauren

4.

Ⓐ Chicago
Ⓑ Rockford
Ⓒ Springfield
Ⓓ Carbondale

STOP

Mathematics: Whole Numbers

This unit of whole numbers covers mathematical skills including:

- grouping tens and ones.
- comparing and ordering numbers; identifying missing numbers.
- estimating using various strategies to determine how many.
- rote counting beyond 100.
- reading and writing word names for numerals.
- counting by twos, fives, and tens.
- naming nearest multiple of 10 on a number line.
- identifying odd and even numbers using objects.
- dividing regions/sets into halves.
- solving problems using addition and subtraction.
- using counting strategies to find sums/differences.
- telling missing addends for addition facts.
- solving three single-digit addition problems.
- solving two-digit addition and subtraction problems.

Teacher Script

Now I am going to ask questions about numbers and counting. I will ask you a question. You will look at the choices, and then fill in the circle of your answer. Let's do a sample question first.

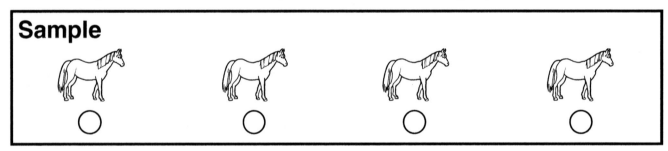

Sample

Look at the four horses standing in a line. (*Make sure students are on the correct page.*) Fill in the circle of the horse that is third in line. (*Pause.*) Which one is third? (*Illustrate on the board.*) Now you will answer some questions on your own. We will not discuss them.

Go to number 1. Here is the question. Which number comes between 7 and 9? (*Pause.*) (*8*)

Now look at number 2. Which number would be next: 4, 6, 8, ___. (*Pause.*) (*10*)

Look at number 3. Which number comes before 13? (*Pause.*) (*12*)

We are on number 4 now. Which number is less than 7? (Pause) (*6*)

Number 5 is next. Look at the picture of the blocks. The tall stack of blocks has 10. The short stack has five. How many blocks are in the picture? (*Pause.*) (*30*)

Go to number 6. Look at the pictures of the blocks. Each stack of blocks has five blocks. Which group has 25 blocks? (*Pause.*) (*the second one*)

Go to number 7. Look at the pictures of the blocks. The tall stacks are groups of five. How many more blocks would you need to make 13? Fill in the circle of your choice. (*Pause.*) (*3*)

Go to number 8. Look at the pictures of the black circles. There are two groups of ten. How many more black circles are needed to make 26? (*Pause.*) (*6*)

Turn the page.

Sample

○   ○   ○   ○

1.

6   **8**   **10**   **11**

○   ○   ○   ○

2.

2   **12**   **10**   **14**

○   ○   ○   ○

3.

14   **15**   **16**   **12**

○   ○   ○   ○

4.

8   **9**   **6**   **7**

○   ○   ○   ○

5.

○ **15**
○ **4**
○ **30**
○ **25**

6.

            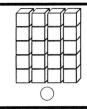

○   ○   ○   ○

7.

○   ○   ○

8.

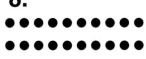

○   ○   ○   ➥

Teacher Script *(cont.)*

Go to number 9. Look at the row of numbers. One of them is missing. Which one? Fill in the circle next to the number that is missing. *(Pause.)* *(105)*

Now go to number 10. There is a missing number in this row of numbers, too. Which one? Fill in the circle next to the number that is missing. *(Pause.)* *(112)*

Now we're on question number 11. There is a missing number in this row of numbers, too. Which one? Fill in the circle next to the number that is missing. *(Pause.)* *(97)*

Go to question number 12. This is a row of numbers. But we are counting by 2s. A number in the row is missing. Which number? Fill in the circle next to the number that is missing. *(Pause.)* *(8)*

We are on question number 13 now. This is another row of numbers. But we are counting by 5s now. A number in the row is missing. Which number? Fill in the circle next to the number that is missing. *(Pause.)* *(10)*

Go to question number 14. This is another row of numbers. But we are counting by 10s now. A number in the row is missing. Which number? Fill in the circle next to the number that is missing. *(Pause.)* *(30)*

Now stop.

ANSWER KEY

1. (8)
2. (10)
3. (12)
4. (6)
5. (30)
6. the second picture
7. (3)
8. (6)
9. (105)
10. (112)
11. (97)
12. (8)
13. (10)
14. (30)

9.

103 104 ___ 106 107

- ◯ 102
- ◯ 107
- ◯ 100
- ◯ 105

10.

111 ___ 113 114 115

- ◯ 110
- ◯ 116
- ◯ 112
- ◯ 100

11.

___ 98 99 100

- ◯ 96
- ◯ 97
- ◯ 90
- ◯ 99

12.

2 4 6 ___

- ◯ 10
- ◯ 12
- ◯ 8
- ◯ 9

13.

5 ___ 15 20

- ◯ 12
- ◯ 10
- ◯ 1
- ◯ 25

14.

10 20 ___ 40

- ◯ 10
- ◯ 30
- ◯ 50
- ◯ 25

Teacher Script

On this test, you will count how many are in a row, and write the word for the number. Here is a sample.

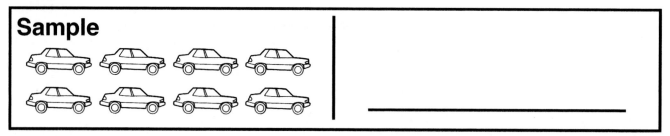

Sample

How many cars are in the race? Count them and write the word for the number on the blank line.

There are eight cars, and you should have written the word for eight on the blank lines. (Write "eight" on the board.) Do not write the number; write the word for the number.

Look at row number 1. Look at the cupcakes. How many cupcakes are there in all? Write the word for the number on the line. *(Pause.)* *(five)*

Go to row number 2. Look at the birds. How many birds are there in all? Write the word for the number on the line. *(Pause.)* *(seven)*

Go to row number 3. Look at the blocks. How many blocks are there in all? Write the word for the number on the line. *(Pause.)* *(six)*

Go to row number 4. Look at the squares. How many squares are there in all? Write the word for the number on the line. *(Pause.)* *(twelve)*

Now go to row number 5. Look at the animals. How many animals are there in all? Write the word for the number on the line. *(Pause.)* *(ten)*

Go to row number 6. Look at the stars. How many stars are there in all? Write the word for the number on the line. *(Pause.)* *(nine)*

Go to row number 7. Look at the birthday cakes. How many are there? Write the word for the number on the line. *(Pause.)* *(four)*

Now we're on the last one, row number 8. Look at the baseball bats. How many are there? Write the word for the number on the line. *(Pause.)* *(eight)*

Now stop.

ANSWER KEY

1. five
2. seven
3. six
4. twelve
5. ten
6. nine
7. four
8. eight

Sample

_____

1.

_____

2.

_____

3.

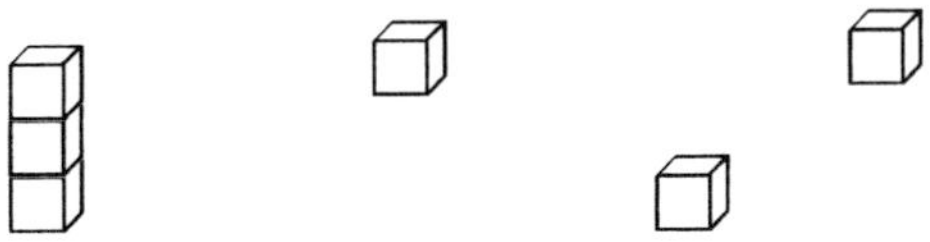

_____

4.

_____

5.

_____

6.
★ ★ ☆ ☆ ☆ ☆ ☆ ★ ★

_____

7.

_____

8.

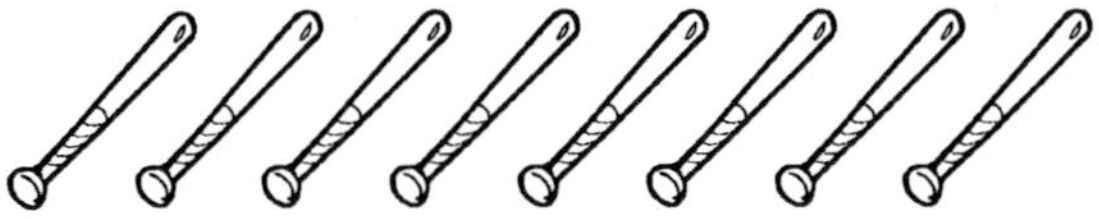

_____

STOP

Teacher Script

Now we are going to make guesses about numbers. The choices are in rows again. I will ask a question, and you will fill in the circle of your answer. First, let's do addition problems. Here is a sample.

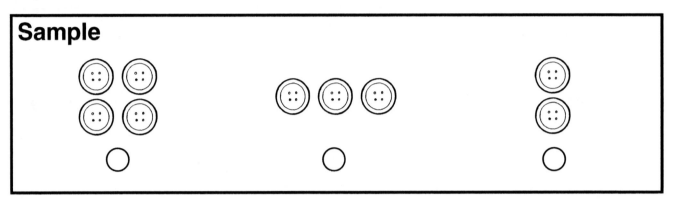

Sample

Kim had two buttons on her dress. Her mother sewed on two more buttons. How many buttons are on Kim's dress now? Fill in the circle of your answer. *(Pause.)* *(four buttons)* *(Draw on the board to illustrate the problem.)*

Now you will answer the addition problems on your own. Listen carefully while I ask each question. We will not discuss the answers.

Put your finger on the number 1. This is the row we are on. Three cars drove into the parking lot. Then three more came. How many cars are in the parking lot now? *(Pause.)* *(six cars)*

Put your finger on the number 2. Mrs. Carter had ten small plants for her garden. Then she bought two more. How many plants does she have in all? *(Pause.)* *(twelve plants)*

Put your finger on the number 3. Two ants crawled out of an anthill. Two more ants crawled out to join them. How many ants crawled out of the hill in all? *(Pause.)* *(four ants)*

Put your finger on the number 4. There were three eggs in a nest. The mother bird laid two more. How many eggs are in the nest? *(Pause.)* *(five eggs)*

Put your finger on the number 5. There were two fish swimming in one bowl and three fish swimming in another bowl. How many fish are swimming in all? *(Pause.)* *(five fish)*

Put your finger on the number 6. One butterfly was on a branch. Two more butterflies flew nearby. How many butterflies were there in all? *(Pause.)* *(three butterflies)*

Now stop.

ANSWER KEY

1. six cars **2.** twelve plants **3.** four ants **4.** five eggs **5.** five fish **6.** three butterflies

---

Sample

1.

2.

3.

4.

5.

6.

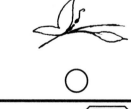

Teacher Script

Now we will do subtraction or take away problems. This part of the test is different from the addition part. The answers will be numbers, not pictures. Here is a sample.

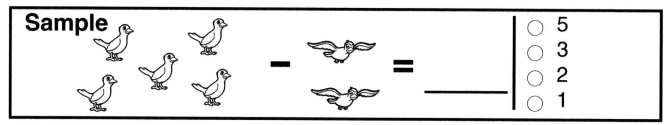

Look at the birds. There were five birds on the ground. Two of the birds flew away. How many birds are left on the ground? Fill in the circle under the number that shows how many birds are left on the ground. *(Pause.)* How many birds were left? *(three)*

Now you will answer questions on your own. Remember, this time the questions are about subtraction or taking away.

Look at the pictures in row number 1. Mario has five pears. He gave three pears to Audrey. How many pears did Mario have left? Fill in the circle under your answer. *(Pause.)* *(2)*

Go to row number 2. Todd gave his dog, Dilly, six dog biscuits. Dilly ate two of them right away. How many biscuits did Dilly have left? *(Pause.)* *(4)*

Now look at number 3. Jason had fourteen cookies in his lunch. If he gave four cookies to his friend, how many cookies would Jason have left? Fill in the circle of your answer. *(Pause.)* *(10)*

See question number 4. Six children were playing in the yard. Two of them went home for lunch. How many children stayed to play in the yard. *(Pause.)* *(4)*

Go to number 5. Howard had fifteen books. He loaned three to his friend Dave. How many books does Howard have left? *(Pause.)* *(12)*

Now look at number 6. Lisa had ten blocks. She stacked up seven of them. How many blocks did Lisa not use in her stack? *(Pause.)* *(3)*

Look at number 7. There are five groups of five blocks each, or 25 blocks in all. If we take away one group of blocks, how many are left? *(Pause.)* *(20)*

Now go to number 8. There are four groups of three stars, or twelve in all. If we take away half of them, how many are left? *(Pause.)* *(6)*

Now stop.

ANSWER KEY
1. (2)
2. (4)
3. (10)
4. (4)
5. (12)
6. (3)
7. (20)
8. (6)

Sample 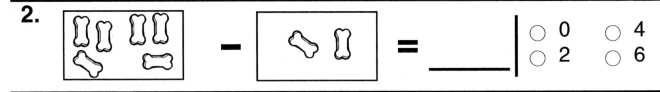 − = _____
- ○ 5
- ○ 3
- ○ 2
- ○ 1

1. − = _____
- ○ 2   ○ 5
- ○ 1   ○ 3

2. − = _____
- ○ 0   ○ 4
- ○ 2   ○ 6

3. − = _____
- ○ 17   ○ 13
- ○ 10   ○ 11

4. − = _____
- ○ 1   ○ 4
- ○ 2   ○ 6

5. − = _____
- ○ 12   ○ 16
- ○ 13   ○ 11

6. − = _____
- ○ 3   ○ 10
- ○ 7   ○ 13

7. − = _____
- ○ 20   ○ 30
- ○ 15   ○ 5

8. = _____
- ○ 9   ○ 5
- ○ 7   ○ 6

STOP

This math skills section covers the following:

- naming nearest multiple of 10 on a number line.
- identifying odd and even numbers, using objects.
- dividing regions/sets into halves.

Teacher Script

Now you will see pictures having to do with numbers. You must listen carefully to my questions so you can choose a good answer. Here is a sample.

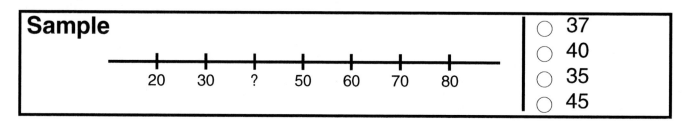

Here is a number line. There are numbers on the line in 10s. Look closely at the number line. See the question mark? There is a number missing there. Which number is it? Fill in the circle next to the answer you choose. *(Pause.)* *(40)*

Now you will answer questions on your own.

Go to number 1. Here is another number line. There are numbers in 5s. Look closely at the number line. See the question mark? There is a number missing there. Which number is it? Fill in the circle next to the answer you choose. *(Pause.)* *(120)*

Now we are at number 2. See the groups of toys. One group has an odd number of toys. Which group has an odd number of toys? Fill in the circle of your answer. *(Pause.)* *(the third picture)*

Go to number 3. Now there are groups of things to eat. One group has an even number of things to eat. Which group has an even number of things to eat? *(Pause.)* *(the second picture)*

Look at number 4 now. Here is a picture of six bicycles. Half of them need to be fixed. If half of them need to be fixed, how many is that? Fill in the circle next to your answer. *(Pause.)* *(3)*

Go to number 5. Now there are four pairs of children. Half of the children are going on a field trip tomorrow. How many children are going on a field trip? *(Pause.)* *(4)*

Go to number 6. Here are sandwiches and plates. There are four sandwiches and four plates. If one sandwich is put on each plate, what will be half the number of sandwiches on plates? *(Pause.)* *(2)*

Now stop.

ANSWER KEY
1. (120)
2. the third picture of toys
3. the second picture of things to eat
4. (3)
5. (4)
6. (2)

Sample

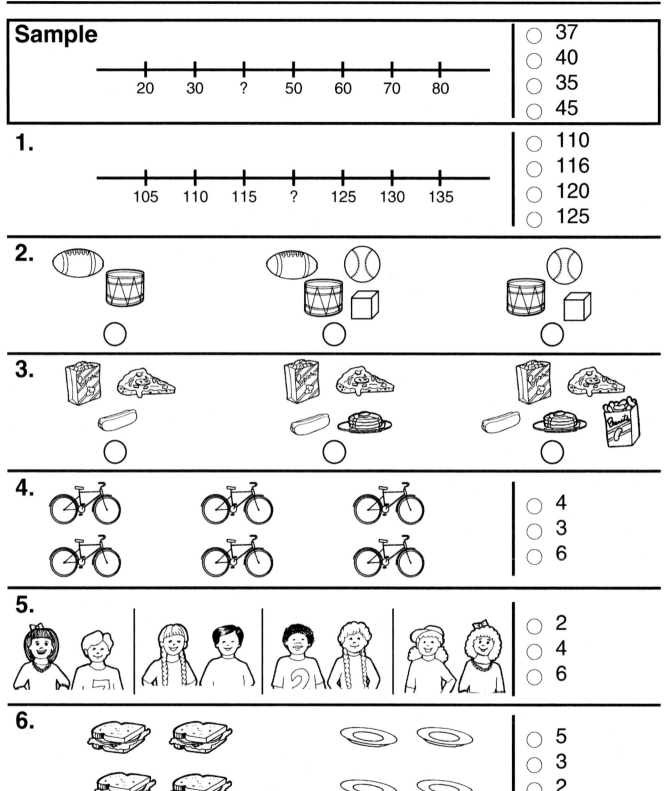

Sample
- ○ 37
- ○ 40
- ○ 35
- ○ 45

1.
- ○ 110
- ○ 116
- ○ 120
- ○ 125

4.
- ○ 4
- ○ 3
- ○ 6

5.
- ○ 2
- ○ 4
- ○ 6

6.
- ○ 5
- ○ 3
- ○ 2

STOP

This second grade math section covers the following:
- telling missing addends for addition facts.
- solving three single-digit addition problems.
- solving two-digit addition and subtraction problems.

Teacher Script

On this page of the test, we will do some more addition and subtraction, but you must listen carefully to my question. Look at the following sample.

Sample

$$5 + X = 9$$

- ○ 3
- ○ 6
- ○ 4

Here is an addition problem, but a number is missing. You can see how much the sum is, but a missing number in the problem is shown as X. How much is X? Fill in the circle of your answer. (*Pause.*) (*4*)

Now you will answer questions on your own.

Go to number 1. Here is another addition problem, but again a number is missing. You can see the sum, but the missing number in the problem is shown as X. How much is X? Fill in the circle of your answer. (*Pause.*) (*3*)

Now we are on number 2. Here is an addition problem. You must solve it on your own. Fill in the circle of your answer. (*Pause.*) (*6*)

Go to number 3. Here is another addition problem. You must solve it on your own. Fill in the circle of your answer. (*Pause.*) (*11*)

Now go to question number 4. Here is an addition problem. You may write on your test if that will help you think. Fill in the circle of your answer. (*Pause.*) (*21*)

Now we are on question number 5. Here is another addition problem. You may write on your test if that will help you think. Fill in the circle of your answer. (*Pause.*) (*28*)

Go to question number 6. This is a subtraction problem this time. You may write on your test if that will help you think. Fill in the circle of your answer. (*Pause.*) (*4*)

We are on number 7 now, the last one in this part of the test. This is also a subtraction problem. You may write on your test if that will help you think. Fill in the circle of your answer. (*Pause.*) (*11*)

Now stop.

ANSWER KEY

1. (3)
2. (6)
3. (11)
4. (21)
5. (28)
6. (4)
7. (11)

Sample		
$5 + X = 9$	○ 3 ○ 6 ○ 4	

1.

$X + 4 = 7$	○ 2 ○ 3 ○ 4

2.

$3 + 2 + 1 =$	○ 6 ○ 5 ○ 7

3.

$5 + 4 + 2 =$	○ 9 ○ 10 ○ 11

4.

$10 + 11 =$	○ 20 ○ 12 ○ 21

5.

$15 + 13 =$	○ 28 ○ 29 ○ 18

6.

$16 - 12 =$	○ 28 ○ 4 ○ 3

7.

$21 - 10 =$	○ 11 ○ 20 ○ 31

STOP

Mathematics: Geometric Ideas

This section of second grade math skills includes the following:
- identifying and making figures with line symmetry.
- matching congruent figures.
- recognizing geometric figures in the environment.

Teacher Script

In this part of the test you will answer questions about shapes. You will be drawing a little, too. Here is a sample. Look at the two shapes. Beside the shapes is a pair of lines. What would you have to add to the lines to make a shape like the other two? Do that now. Draw right on your page. (*Pause.*)

Sample

Did you add lines like this? (*Illustrate on the board adding a top and bottom line to make a complete square.*) Yes, adding these lines would make a shape like the other two. You will be answering problems like this on this part of the test.

Find number 1. Here are two shapes that are the same. Add a line to the third shape to make it like the other two. Do that now. Draw right on your page. (*Pause.*) (*A third line must be added to make a third triangle.*)

We are on question number 2 now. Here are two shapes. In the middle are two lines. What would have to be added to the lines to make a shape like the other two? Do that now. Draw right on your page. (*Pause.*) (*Two sides of the trapezoid must be added.*)

Go to question number 3. Here is a shape. Listen carefully. If you put a mirror on the line, then what shape would you see? Fill in the bubble for what you would see. (*Pause.*) (*A complete heart with a line down the center.*)

Go to question number 4. Here is a shape. Fill in the bubble for another shape that is the same. (*Pause.*) (*the third one*)

Go to number 5. Look at the suitcase. Which word describes the shape of the suitcase? Fill in the bubble. (*Pause.*) (*rectangle*)

Go to number 6. Look at the pictures of the mat, the book, and the board game. With which group of shapes do they belong? Fill in the bubble for your answer. (*Pause.*) (*rectangles*)

Now go to number 7. This is the last one on this page. Here is a group of four small squares that are partly black and partly white. Next is another group of only three squares. Choose a square that would make both groups the same. (*Pause.*) (*the second one*)

Now stop.

ANSWER KEY

1. third line added to triangle
2. two sides of the trapezoid must be added
3. a complete heart with a line down the center
4. the third picture

5. rectangle
6. rectangles
7. the second picture

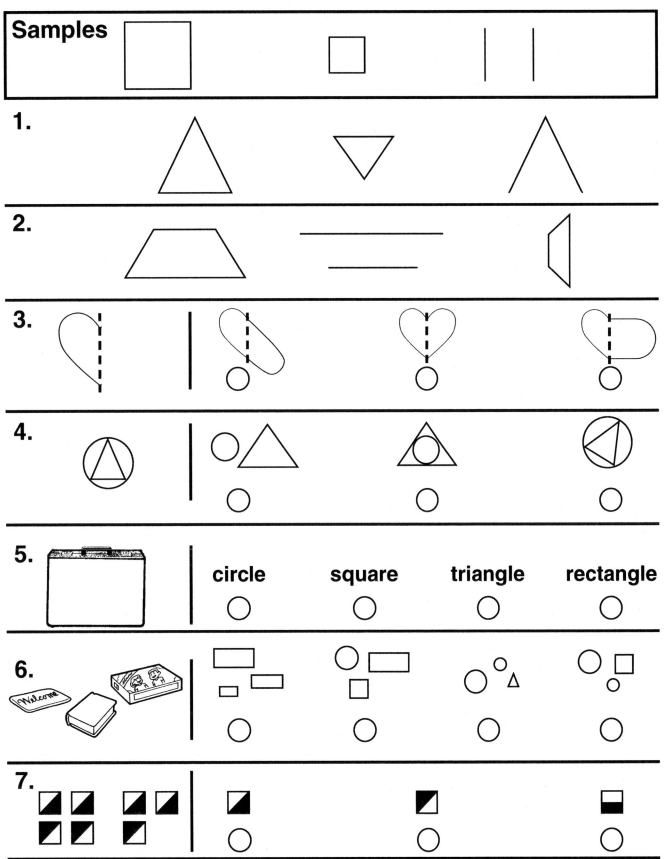

Samples

1.

2.

3.

4.

5. circle   square   triangle   rectangle

6.

7.

Mathematics: Classification and Pattern

This section of second grade math skills includes the following:

- comparing and describing similarities and differences.
- classifying by more than one attribute.
- defining and continuing patterns.
- identifying classification and patterning in the environment.
- continuing patterns of numerical sequences.
- finding and correcting errors in patterns.
- ordering objects and events.

Teacher Script

Put your finger on the number 1. Look at the pictures. You see these things in the world. Which one has a pattern? Fill in the circle of your answer. (*Pause.*) (*railroad tracks*)

Go to the number 2. Here is a picture of the pyramids in Egypt. If another one were going to be built, what shape would it have? Fill in the circle under your answer. (*Pause.*) (*triangle*)

Look at the number 3. Here is a picture of the back of an envelope. What shapes do the lines make? (*Pause.*) (*triangles*)

Find the number 4. Which of these has a pattern? Fill in the circle of your answer. (*Pause.*) (*soccer ball*)

Put your finger on the number 5. One of these pictures does not belong. Which one? (*Pause.*) (*coin*)

Look at the number 6. One of these pictures does not belong. Which one? (*Pause.*) (*carrot*)

We are on now on number 7. Here is a pattern of numbers. Which numbers would come next in the pattern? Fill in the circle of your answer. (*Pause*) (*6, 5*)

Turn the page.

1.
○　　　○　　　○　　　○

2. 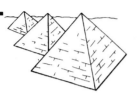 |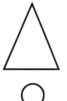
　　　○　　　○　　　○　　　○

3. 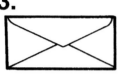 |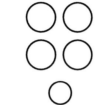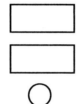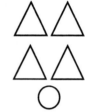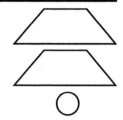
　　　○　　　○　　　○　　　○

4.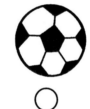
○　　　○　　　○　　　○

5.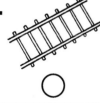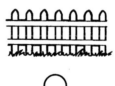
○　　　○　　　○　　　○

6.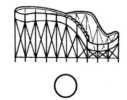
○　　　○　　　○　　　○

7.

$$3, 2 \qquad 4, 3 \qquad 5, 4 \qquad \_\_\_$$

- ○ 5, 6
- ○ 6, 5
- ○ 3, 4

Teacher Script *(cont.)*

Go to number 8. Here is another pattern of numbers. Which numbers would come next in the pattern? Fill in the circle of your answer. *(Pause.)* *(9, 12, 15)*

Go to number 9. In this pattern of numbers there is a mistake. Which number does not belong? Fill in the circle of your answer. *(Pause.)* *(10)*

Go to number 10. Here is a pattern of numbers. Which number belongs in the blank? *(Pause.)* *(6)*

Now we are on number 11. Here are some dice all in a row. To continue the pattern, which die should come next? Fill in the circle next to your answer. *(Pause.)* *(the die with four dots)*

Go to number 12. Look at the pictures about baking a cake. Which one comes first? *(Pause.)* *(the second one)*

Go to number 13. Look at the pictures about painting. Which happened last? *(Pause.)* *(complete clown face)*

Go to number 14, the last one. Listen to what a boy said. He said, "We laughed during the puppet show." Which picture is during the puppet show? *(Pause.)* *(the first picture)*

Now stop.

ANSWER KEY

1. railroad tracks **2.** triangle **3.** triangles **4.** soccer ball **5.** coin **6.** carrot **7.** (6, 5)
8. (9, 12, 15) **9.** (10) **10.** (6) **11.** the die with four dots **12.** second picture
13. complete clown face **14.** first picture

Mathematics: Classification and Pattern *(cont.)*

8.

0, 3, 6, 3, 6, 9, 6, 9, 12

- ◯ 9, 12, 13
- ◯ 3, 6, 15
- ◯ 9, 12, 15

9.

2, 5, 3, 5, 4, 5, 10

- ◯ 4
- ◯ 5
- ◯ 10

10.

6/3, 8/4, 10/5, 12/___

- ◯ 12
- ◯ 10
- ◯ 6

11.

   ___

- ◯
- ◯
- ◯

12.

◯   ◯   ◯   ◯

13.

   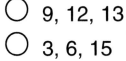

◯   ◯   ◯   ◯

14.

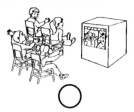  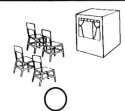

◯   ◯   ◯

STOP

Mathematics: Metric and Customary Measurement

This section of second grade math skills includes the following:

- estimating one inch and one centimeter.
- measuring capacity to the nearest cup.
- estimating number of smaller units contained in a larger unit.
- reading Celsius and Fahrenheit thermometers.
- choosing an appropriate tool for measuring.

- sequencing months.
- telling time to nearest half hour.
- giving value of sets of coins.
- making change using coins.
- solving simple time/money questions.
- locating points on a number line.

Teacher Script

In this part of the test, you will answer questions about measurement, time, and money. Here is a sample.

Sample		3 lbs.	4 lbs.	5 lbs.	6 lbs.
		○	○	○	○

Look at the picture of the scale with a rock on it. How much does the rock weigh? Fill in the circle of your answer.

The pointer is at 4, isn't it? (*discussion*) The rock weighs 4 pounds. You will also be asked questions about calendars and coins. Listen carefully to the questions as I read them.

Go to question number 1. There is a picture of a ruler. How many inches are on this ruler? Fill in the circle of your answer. (*Pause.*) (*4 inches*)

Now go to question number 2. Here are three black lines. Which one looks about as long as a centimeter? Fill in the circle next to your answer. (*Pause.*) (*the first one*)

Now go to number 3. A case of soda pop has four six-packs of pop in it. How many cans of pop are in a case? (*Pause.*) (*24*)

Now go to number 4. Look at the picture of the box. Which is the only other box that will fit inside it? (*Pause.*) (*the smallest one*)

We are on number 5. Look at the picture of the shape. Which is the only other shape that will fit inside of it? (*Pause.*) (*the cone*)

Go to question number 6. Here are two thermometers. Both are showing the temperature at which water freezes, but one is a Celsius thermometer. Which one is a Celsius thermometer? Fill in the circle next to the one you choose. (*Pause.*) (*the left one*)

Go to number 7, the last one. Which tool would you choose for measuring height? Fill in the circle next to your answer. (*Pause.*) (*the ruler*)

Now stop.

ANSWER KEY

1. 4 inches

2. the first picture

3. (24)

4. the smallest box

5. the cone (third picture)

6. the left thermometer

7. the ruler

Mathematics: Metric and Customary Measurement (cont.)

Sample

3 lbs. ○   4 lbs. ○   5 lbs. ○   6 lbs. ○

1.

○ 16 inches   ○ 4 inches
○ 1 inches   ○ 6 inches

2.

— ○   — ○   — ○

3.

12 ○   **16** ○   **20** ○   **24** ○

4.

○   ○   ○   ○

5.

○   ○   ○   ○

6.

○   ○

7.

○   ○   ○   ○

STOP

Teacher Script

Now let's talk about months and days. Go to number 1. Here are some of the months of the year in order. But which month is missing? Fill in the circle of your choice. *(Pause.)* *(August)*

Now go to number 2. Here is the question. Listen carefully. What month comes after October? *(Pause.)* *(November)*

Now look at number 3. Here are some of the days of the week in order. One is missing. Which one? *(Pause.)* *(Thursday)*

Go to number 4. Here are pictures of four clocks. Which one shows the time of 10 o'clock? *(Pause.)* *(first one)*

You should be on number 5 now. There are two kinds of clocks: those with round faces and those that show just numbers. Look at the picture of the round clock. What time is it showing in numbers? *(Pause.)* *(3:30)*

Go to question number 6. Listen to my little story. Heather was supposed to arrive at her grandmother's house at two o'clock. She was a half-hour late. What time did she arrive? Fill in the circle next to the clock that shows the time she arrived. *(Pause.)* *(2:30)*

Turn the page.

Mathematics: Metric and Customary Measurement (cont.)

1.

June, July, _____, September, October

- ◯ May
- ◯ August
- ◯ March
- ◯ December

2.

December   September   November   January

◯   ◯   ◯   ◯

3.

Tuesday, Wednesday, _____, Friday

- ◯ Thursday
- ◯ Monday
- ◯ Saturday
- ◯ Sunday

4.

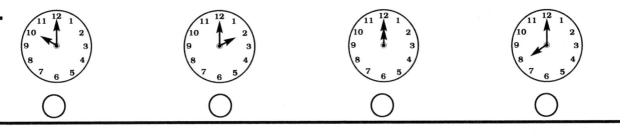

◯   ◯   ◯   ◯

5.

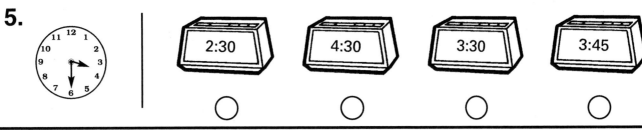

| 2:30 | 4:30 | 3:30 | 3:45 |

◯   ◯   ◯   ◯

6.

◯   ◯   ◯   ◯

Teacher Script

This is a calendar for one month of the year. I am going to ask you some questions about the calendar.

Put your finger on the number 7. For which month is this calendar? *(Pause.)* *(March)*

Put your finger on the number 8. On which day of the week does this month begin? *(Pause.)* *(Monday)*

Put your finger on the number 9. On which day of the week is the 12th? *(Pause.)* *(Friday)*

Put your finger on the number 10. How many days are in this month? *(Pause.)* *(31)*

Now stop.

ANSWER KEY

1. August

2. November

3. Thursday

4. the first clock

5. (3:30)

6. the third clock

7. March

8. Monday

9. Friday

10. (31)

March						
Sun.	Mon.	Tues.	Wed.	Thurs.	Fri.	Sat.
	1	2	3	4	5	6
7	8	9	10	11	12	13
14	15	16	17	18	19	20
21	22	23	24	25	26	27
28	29	30	31			

7.

Mon.	March	Fri.	Sat.
◯	◯	◯	◯

8.

Sun.	Sat.	Wed.	Mon.
◯	◯	◯	◯

9.

Wed.	Thurs.	Fri.	Sat.
◯	◯	◯	◯

10.

28	**29**	**30**	**31**
◯	◯	◯	◯

STOP

Mathematics: Metric and Customary Measurement *(cont.)*

Teacher Script

Go to question number 1. Look at these coin groups. Which group is closest in amount to one dollar? (*Pause.*) (*second group*)

Go to question number 2. Look at the four groups of coins. Fill in the circle under the group that is worth the most money. (*Pause.*) (*second group*)

Now we are on question number 3. This is a question about making change. Pretend that the coins are a subtraction problem. Fill the circle next to your answer. (*Pause.*) (*a nickel*)

Now we are on question number 4. This is another question about making change. Pretend that the coins are a subtraction problem. Fill the circle next to your answer. (*Pause.*) (*a dime*)

Now go to number 5. This is a story problem. You must listen to the story to choose the answer. Two girls were selling lemonade on a hot day. "Five cents! Five cents!" they called. A thirsty runner stopped and said, "I have a dime." "OK," they said. And they gave him a glass of lemonade. Which coin did they give him in change? (*Pause.*) (*a nickel*)

Now go to question number 6. Here is a picture of a number line. Each mark between the 10s is one. To what number is the arrow pointing? (*Pause.*) (*22*)

Now go to question number 7. Here is another picture of a number line. Each mark between the numbers is one. To what number is the arrow pointing to? (*Pause.*) (*17*)

Now stop.

ANSWER KEY

1. second group

2. second group

3. a nickel

4. a dime

5. a nickel

6. (22)

7. (17)

---

1. ◯ ◯ ◯ ◯

2. ◯ ◯ ◯ ◯

3. 🪙 **—** 🪙 **=** _____
- ◯ 1 dime
- ◯ 1 quarter
- ◯ 4 pennies
- ◯ 1 nickel

4. 🪙 **—** 🪙 **=** _____
- ◯ 1 nickel
- ◯ 1 dime
- ◯ 3 nickels
- ◯ 1 quarter

5. ◯ ◯ ◯ ◯

6.

```
  0    10   20   30   40
```
- ◯ 12
- ◯ 22
- ◯ 23
- ◯ 21

7.

```
  0    5    10   15   20   25
```
- ◯ 15
- ◯ 19
- ◯ 14
- ◯ 17

STOP

This section includes the following important problem-solving skills:

- solving spatial visualization puzzles.

- estimating reasonable solutions.

- solving simple logic problems.

- using diagrams or lists to solve problems.

Teacher Script

Do you know what a puzzle is? What is a puzzle? *(discussion)* What makes a puzzle fun to do? *(discussion)* In this part of the book, you will be answering questions that are like puzzles. Here is a sample at the top of your page. Here is a triangle. Look at the row of four black shapes next to it. Which shape is like the triangle? Fill in the circle of your answer. *(Pause.)* Which one did you choose? *(upside-down triangle)* Why? *(discussion)* Now you will do some of these puzzles on your own. Listen carefully.

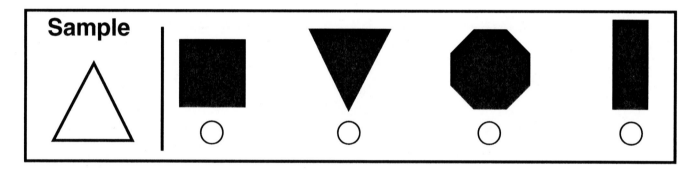

Put your finger on the number 1. Look at the pictures. If these things were in alphabetical order, which one would be first? Fill in the circle under your answer. *(Pause.)* *(the balloon)*

Put your finger on the number 2. Look at the pictures. Now, if these pictures were in alphabetical order, which one would be last? *(Pause.)* *(the zebra)*

Put your finger on the number 3. Listen to my question. There are three pictures this time. If they were in alphabetical order, which one would be in the middle? *(Pause.)* *(the dress)*

Put your finger on the number 4. Look at the picture of the shape that looks like a C. Which one of the other shapes looks like it? Fill in the circle under your answer. *(Pause.)* *(the fourth shape)*

Put your finger on the number 5. Look at the four shapes. Pretend they are being cut where the dotted lines are. If you cut them on the dotted lines, which one will make two triangles? *(Pause.)* *(the fourth picture)*

Put your finger on the number 6. Here is another question about cutting. Look at the four pictures. If you cut the shapes on the dotted lines, which one will make two equal parts? *(Pause.)* *(the square)*

Turn the page.

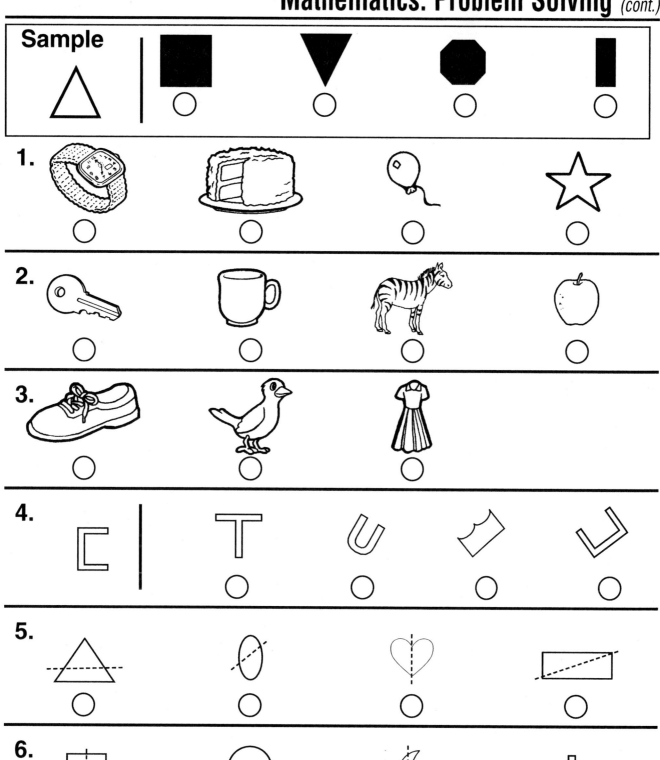

Teacher Script *(cont.)*

Go to number 7. Look at the picture of the scissors cutting a piece of paper. What shape will the scissors cut out? *(Pause.)* *(triangle)*

Go to question number 8. For this question, you must listen to choose an answer. If you saved $5.15 for a gift, and the gift cost $10, about how much more money do you need to save? Fill in the circle of the best answer. *(Pause.)* *($5.00)*

Go to question number 9. Listen to my question. In six months, Jessica's baby sister will be one year old. How old is Jessica's sister now? *(Pause.)* *(6 months old)*

Go to number 10. Now you must look at a chart. This is a chart of books read in a second grade reading group. Look at the chart. Who read the most books? *(Pause.)* *(Andrew)*

Now we are number 11, the last one in this section. Look at the chart again. Who read the same number of books? *(Pause.)* *(Kyle and Heidi)*

Now stop.

ANSWER KEY

1. balloon
2. zebra
3. dress
4. the fourth shape
5. the fourth picture
6. square
7. triangle
8. $5.00
9. 6 months old
10. Andrew
11. Kyle and Heidi

7.

○   ○   ○   ○

8.

$6.00 $5.00 $10.00

○   ○   ○

9.

6 months old   1 year old   1½ year old

○   ○   ○

10.

Name	Books Read
Holly	6
Tiffany	4
Lauren	7
Kristin	3
Kyle	5
Heidi	5
Andrew	8
Dustin	2

Holly   **Lauren**   **Andrew**

○   ○   ○

11.

Holly and Tiffany   **Kyle and Heidi**   **Andrew and Holly**

○   ○   ○

This computer/technology section includes the following:

- identifying uses of technology in the community.

- recognizing a person's rights of ownership of computer-related work, and responsible behavior when using computers.

- identifying how telecommunications has changed the ways people work and play.

Teacher Script

In this part of the test, we are going to talk about how we use computers and technology. You know what a computer is, but what is technology? Can you give me some examples? (*discussion*) Technology is using machines and tools to help us with the work we do.

Look at the page, you will see three pictures in each row of people at work and play. One of the pictures will show someone using technology. Fill in the circle next to picture of someone using technology. (*Allow students several minutes to complete the page silently.*)

Now stop.

ANSWER KEY

1. boy at computer

2. someone driving a car

3. playing a computer game

4. people at a movie

5. boy using video camera

6. worker using a bulldozer

7. news on TV

1.

2.

3.

4.

5.

6.

7.

STOP

Teacher Script

On this page, we will talk about two things: respecting people's computer property and behaving responsibly around computers. I will tell you a story about a class of second graders. Listen carefully.

Mrs. Johnson's second grade class uses computers almost everyday. They write stories; they e-mail children at another school; they look for information. Mrs. Johnson has the following rules about using computers:

- Respect other people.
- Do not steal.
- Do not waste.
- Do not lie.
- Do not destroy.

(Write all the rules on the board.)

Mrs. Johnson's class usually obeys the rules. But sometimes, a student will break one of the rules. I am going to tell you about what some students did. You will decide which rule was broken. Here is a sample. Listen to this little story.

"One day, just for fun, Tamika set the printer on 100 copies. Then she left her seat at the computer. No one knew who made 100 copies."

Which rule did Tamika break? Fill in the circle next to your answer.

Sample

Do not steal.   ◯   **Do not waste.**   ◯   **Respect other people.**   ◯

Which did you choose? *(discussion)* Yes, she broke the rule "Do not waste." No one needed 100 copies, and so much time and paper was used up for nothing.

Now you will hear other examples of students breaking the rules. You will choose which rule in Mrs. Johnson's class was broken.

Go to number 1. Arthur is angry at Jason. He took Jason's disk and erased it. Then he put it back on Jason's desk and said nothing. Which rule was broken? *(Do not destroy.)*

Go to number 2. Angela found a good story on her computer that someone else had written. She copied it, put her name at the top, and handed it in. *(Do not lie or do not steal.)*

Now we are on number 3. Paul does not like a boy in another class. He sends messages to the other boy's computer everyday, making fun of him. Which rule is being broken? *(Respect other people.)*

Now we are on number 4. Tommy borrows Spencer's game disks. He makes copies of them at home. He tells Spencer he will erase the game if he does not like it, or buy the game if he does. What rule is being broken? *(Do not steal primarily; Do not lie, but that is an assumption.)*

Go to question number 5. Sandra writes to students at other schools on her computer. She tells them that she is the teacher and pretends that she is. What rule is being broken? *(Do not lie.)*

Go to question number 6. This is the last story. Susan is writing a private journal on her computer. She only wants her teacher, Mrs. Johnson, to see it. But Vanessa keeps looking over Susan's shoulder and telling other students what Susan is writing. What rule is being broken? *(Respect other people.)* Now stop.

ANSWER KEY

1. Do not destroy. **2.** Do not lie or do not steal. **3.** Respect other people. **4.** Do not steal primarily; do not lie, but that is an assumption. **5.** Do not lie. **6.** Respect other people.

Sample

Do not steal.	Do not waste.	Respect other people.
◯	◯	◯

1.

Do not waste.	Do not lie.	Do not destroy.
◯	◯	◯

2.

Do not destroy.	Do not lie.	Do not steal.
◯	◯	◯

3.

Respect other people.	Do not lie.	Do not waste.
◯	◯	◯

4.

Do not steal.	Do not lie.	Do not waste.
◯	◯	◯

5.

Respect other people.	Do not lie.	Do not destroy.
◯	◯	◯

6.

Do not destroy.	Do not waste.	Respect other people.
◯	◯	◯

STOP

Computer/Technology: Knowledge and Skills

This computer/technology section includes the following skills:

- identifying the function of the physical components of a computer system.
- identifying essential computer terms.
- identifying word processing steps.

Teacher Script

In this part of the test about computers and technology, you will identify the main parts of a computer and the special words you use on a computer. I will ask you a question, and you will fill in the circle next to the picture I am talking about.

Go to number 1. Which part of the computer do you use to move the cursor on the screen and click? Fill in the circle under the picture that I am talking about. (*Pause.*) (*the mouse*)

Go to number 2. What part of the computer do you look at while your are writing? (*Pause.*) (*the monitor*)

Now we are on number 3. When a message appears on the computer screen, what does it look like? (*Pause.*) (*the window with instructions*)

Now go to number 4. What do you use to write with on the computer screen? (*Pause.*) (*the keyboard*)

Look at number 5. What do you use to store your work on? (*Pause.*) (*a disk*)

Go to number 6. When you want a paper copy of your work, what does the paper come out of? (*Pause.*) (*a printer*)

Go to number 7. When you want to keep a copy of your writing on a disk, or on the computer, what word do you choose on the screen? (*Pause.*) (*Save*)

Go to number 8. When you want to end what you are doing on the computer, what word do you choose on the screen? (*Pause.*) (*Close or Exit*)

Now stop.

ANSWER KEY

1. mouse
2. monitor
3. window with instructions
4. keyboard
5. disk
6. printer
7. Save
8. Close or Exit

1.

○   ○   ○

2.

○   ○   ○

3.

○   ○   ○

4.

○   ○   ○

5.

○   ○   ○

6.

○   ○   ○

7.

Don't Save	**Save**	**Open**
○	○	○

8.

Close or Exit	**Paste**	**Copy**
○	○	○

Science: Process

This science section includes the following second grade skills:

- making observations based on the five senses.
- classifying objects according to their properties.
- using amounts as a means of quantifying.
- estimating length, volume, mass, and temperature.
- making inferences to form conclusions.
- making predictions.
- using space-time relations.
- making reasonable interpretations from data.

Teacher Script

Now we are on the science part of the test. The questions I will ask you will have to do with temperature, size, and things you notice about the world. There is a sample question at the top of your page.

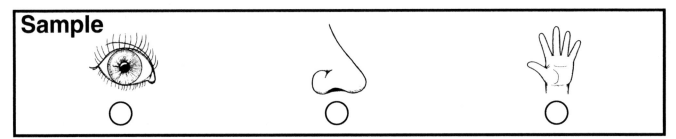

Sample

Listen to my question. You can tell that something is hot or cold by using what part of your body? Fill in the circle under your answer. (*Pause.*) Which answer did you choose? (*hand*) Why? (*discussion*) This part of the book has questions like that.

Go to question number 1. In this row, there are three pictures. Which one is the tallest? Fill in the circle of your answer. (*Pause.*) (*the door*)

Question number 2. In this row there are also three pictures. Which one is the longest? (*Pause.*) (*snake*)

Now question number 3. Look at these pictures. Which one do you think is the hardest? (*Pause.*) (*rock*)

Go to number 4. Here are three pictures of a rocks being weighed on a scale. Look carefully at the pictures. Which rock is the heaviest? Fill in the circle under your answer. (*Pause.*) (*third one*)

Question number 5. Now we are going to compare temperatures. Here are three thermometers. Which one shows the highest temperature? (*Pause.*) (*second one*)

Now we are on number 6. Here is one more question about temperature. Here are pictures of ice, fire, and a glass of water. Which one would have the lowest temperature? (*Pause.*) (*ice*)

Turn the page.

Sample

○ ○ ○

1.

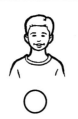 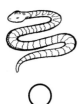

○ ○ ○

2.

○ ○ ○

3.

 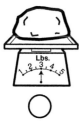 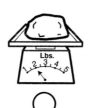 

○ ○ ○

4.

○ ○ ○

5.

○ ○ ○

6.

○ ○ ○

Teacher Script *(cont.)*

Question number 7. Here are three boxes. Pretend that you want to save some crayons in one of these boxes. Which box would hold the most crayons? *(Pause.)* *(first box)*

Now we are on question number 8. Each of these things has water in it. Which one would have the most water? *(Pause.)* *(fish tank)*

Go to number 9. Now I am going to tell you a little story. You must guess what happened in the story. I was having a cold drink with ice one hot, summer day. I left my drink on the table outside. When I came back, the ice was gone. What happened to the ice? Choose the picture that shows what happened. *(Pause.)* *(the ice melting)*

Go to number 10. Here is another story. I bought a balloon. It floated and pulled a little on its string. Then, by accident, I let the string go. What happened to the balloon? Fill in the circle under your answer. *(Pause.)* *(balloon floating away)*

Go to number 11. Here is a picture of a fish bowl half-filled with water. Then, for a joke, someone dropped a ball inside the fishbowl. Which picture shows what the fishbowl would look like after the ball has been dropped in it? *(Pause.)* *(water level is higher)*

Now we are on number 12. Here is another story. Angela was making muffins. She poured them in a muffin tray and put tray in the oven. But she didn't turn the oven on. What will the muffins look like when she takes them out? *(Pause.)* *(second picture)*

Turn the page.

7.

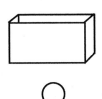 ○   ○   ○

8.

 ○    ○   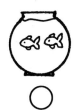 ○

9.

 ○   ○   ○

10.

 ○    ○    ○

11.

 |  ○    ○   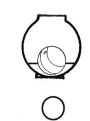 ○

12.

 ○   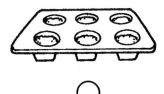 ○    ○

Teacher Script *(cont.)*

Go to question number 13. Here is a little story. You must listen carefully. Andrew came running down the street. "I could tell you were baking cookies," he told his mom. "How could you tell?" said his mother, "You were so far away." How could Andrew tell his mother was baking cookies? Fill in the circle of your answer. *(Pause.)* *(nose)*

Now we are on question number 14. Here is another little story. Lauren said to Kristen, "Let's go! The parade is starting." Kristen said, "How do you know? I can't see it coming." How did Lauren know the parade was coming? *(Pause.)* *(ear)*

Question number 15. Here is one more little story. Kyle and Luke were hiking. Kyle said, "I don't think I want to go to that hill over there. It's too far." Luke said, "How do you know it's far? You've never been there." How did Kyle know it was far to the hill? *(Pause.)* *(eye)*

This is question number 16. Here is a picture of a thermometer. Then there are three more pictures of the thermometer. Which one shows the change in the thermometer's reading after it has been put in a bucket of ice? *(Pause.)* *(the second picture)*

Go to question number 17. Here is another story. Mr. Anderson's class is finding out information. They are finding out which colors of jellybeans are most often found in a one-pound bag of jellybeans. Look at the graph on your page. It shows the results of what the class found. Which color jellybean was found the most often? Fill in the circle of your answer. *(Pause.)* *(red)*

Go to question number 18. Look at the picture again. Which color jellybean was found the least number of times? *(Pause.)* *(black)*

Now stop.

ANSWER KEY

1. door 2. snake 3. rock 4. third picture 5. second thermometer 6. ice 7. first box
8. fish tank (second picture) 9. ice melting 10. balloon floating away (second picture)
11. water level is higher (second picture) 12. uncooked muffins (second picture)
13. nose 14. ear 15. eye 16. the thermometer reading 30 degrees (second picture)
17. red 18. black

13.

○   ○   ○

14.

○   ○   ○

15.

○   ○   ○

16.

○   ○   ○

black ⎯ ⎯ ⎯ ⎯ ⎯
green ⎯ ⎯ ⎯ ⎯ ⎯ ⎯ ⎯
red   ⎯ ⎯ ⎯ ⎯ ⎯ ⎯ ⎯ ⎯ ⎯ ⎯ ⎯ ⎯
yellow ⎯ ⎯ ⎯ ⎯ ⎯ ⎯ ⎯
white ⎯ ⎯ ⎯ ⎯ ⎯ ⎯ ⎯ ⎯ ⎯ ⎯ ⎯
orange ⎯ ⎯ ⎯ ⎯ ⎯ ⎯ ⎯ ⎯

      10   **20**   **30**   **40**   **50**

17.

yellow	red	white
○	○	○

18.

black	green	red
○	○	○

STOP

Social Studies: Citizenship, Authority, and Responsibility

This social studies section includes the following skills:

- identifying attributes of good citizenship.
- describing appropriate behaviors in various environments.
- identifying individuals who have authority.
- recognizing consequences of responsible and irresponsible actions.

Teacher Script

This is the social studies part of the test. In this part there will be questions about living in the United States. Here is a sample. Which is the flag of the United States of America?

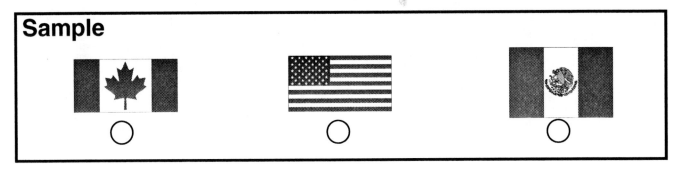

Which one did you choose? (*discussion*) Now you will be asked more questions like that one.

Go to question number 1. Which picture shows boys and girls saying the Pledge of Allegiance? (*Pause.*) (*the third picture*)

Go to number 2. Which picture shows a person being a good citizen on election day? (*Pause.*) (*person voting*)

Go to question number 3. Which picture shows a boy using his hat the right way when the United States flag is raised? (*Pause.*) (*boy with hat off*)

We are on question number 4 now. Which picture show someone being a good citizen in the community? (*Pause.*) (*person cleaning up litter*)

Go to question number 5. Which picture shows children coming into school the right way? (*Pause.*) (*children in a line*)

Go to question number 6. Which words are at the beginning of the National Anthem, the song of our country? Fill in the circle by your answer. (*Pause.*) (*"O, say can you see?"*)

Social Studies: Citizenship, Authority, and Responsibility *(cont.)*

Sample

1.

2.

3.

4.

5.

6. "Columbia, the gem of the ocean"   "Mine eyes have seen the glory . . ."   "O, say can you see?"

Teacher Script (cont.)

Now we will answer some questions about people we must obey and about safe and unsafe behavior.

Go to number 7. Look at the pictures of the three adults. Which one is a referee who makes sure a game is played fairly? (*Pause.*) (*second picture*)

Now number 8. Look at the pictures. Which one is a police car? (*Pause.*) (*the first one*)

Question number 9. Listen to my question. Which picture shows a man who is a leader of a church? (*Pause.*) (*third picture*)

Question number 10. Here are three pictures of children doing things. Which picture shows children being safe? (*Pause.*) (*second picture*)

Go to number 11. Here are three more pictures of children doing things. Which picture shows children being unsafe? (*Pause.*) (*third picture*)

Go to question number 12. Look at these pictures of children. Which one shows a child disobeying? (*Pause.*) (*first picture*)

ANSWER KEY

1. the third picture
2. person voting (first picture)
3. boy with hat off (second picture)
4. person cleaning up (first picture)
5. children in a line (second picture)
6. "O, say can you see?"
7. second picture
8. first picture
9. third picture
10. second picture
11. third picture
12. first picture

7.

○   ○   ○

8.

○   ○   ○

9.

○   ○   ○

10.

○   ○   ○

11.

○   ○   ○

12.

○   ○   ○

STOP

Social Studies: Religious and Cultural Traditions

This social studies section includes the following:

- identifying religious and secular symbols.
- identifying symbols associated with holidays.
- identifying selected famous people in history.

Teacher Script

Now we need to think about our country and how we live in the United States.

Go to number 1. Which is the picture of the first president, George Washington? (*Pause.*) (*third picture*)

Go to number 2. Here are some things used for celebrations. One of them is used by people who are Jewish to celebrate Hanukkah. Which one? (*Pause.*) (*first picture*)

Now question number 3. Which pictures shows what people do with their hands when they pray? (*Pause.*) (*second picture*)

Look at number 4. Here are more pictures of hands. Which one shows people shaking hands? (*Pause.*) (*first picture*)

Now question number 5. There is a famous statue in the United States called the Statue of Liberty. Which picture shows the Statue of Liberty? (*Pause.*) (*third picture*)

Go to question number 6. Our country has a national bird. This bird symbolizes courage and freedom. Which picture shows this bird? (*Pause.*) (*third picture*)

We are on question number 7 now. Here are pictures of three famous Americans. One was a leader who fought for fairness among Americans of all races. Which one is he? Fill in the circle of your answer. (*Pause.*) (*Dr. Martin Luther King, Jr.*)

We are on question number 8 now. On the blank line, write the name of the person who is president of the United States now. Try your best. (*Pause.*)

Now stop.

ANSWER KEY

1. George Washington (third picture) **2.** menorah (first picture) **3.** praying hands (second picture) **4.** shaking hands (first picture) **5.** Statue of Liberty (third picture) **6.** bald eagle (third picture) **7.** Dr. Martin Luther King, Jr. (first picture) **8.** name of current president

---

Social Studies: Religious and Cultural Traditions *(cont.)*

1.

○   ○   ○

2.

○   ○   ○

3.

○   ○   ○

4.

○   ○   ○

5.

○   ○   ○

6.

○   ○   ○

7. Dr. Martin Luther King, Jr.   John Fitzgerald Kennedy   Richard M. Nixon

○   ○   ○

8.

_____

STOP

Tips for Parents: Help Your Child to Write Well

Children must be ready to learn from the first day of school. Preparing children for school is a historic responsibility of parents.

Should you help your child with writing? Yes, if you want your child to do well in school, enjoy self-expression, and become more self-reliant. You know how important writing will be to your child's life. It will be important from first grade through college and throughout adulthood. After all, writing is . . .

Practical

Most of us make lists, jot down reminders, and write notes and instructions at least occasionally.

Job-Related

Professional and white-collar workers write frequently—preparing memos, letters, briefing papers, sales reports, articles, research reports, or proposals. Most workers do some kind of writing on the job.

Stimulating

Writing helps to provoke thoughts and to organize them logically and concisely.

Social

Most of us—at least occasionally—write thank-you notes and letters to friends.

Therapeutic

It can be helpful to express feelings in writing that cannot be expressed so easily by speaking.

How You Can Help

1. **Encourage your child to draw and to discuss his or her drawings.** One of the first means of communication for your child is through drawing. Ask questions such as the following: *What is the boy doing? Does the house look like ours? Can you tell a story about this picture?*

2. **Show an interest in and ask questions about the things your child says, draws, and may try to write.** Most children's basic speech patterns are formed by the time they enter school. By that time, children speak clearly, recognize most letters of the alphabet, and may try to write.

3. **Make it real.** Your child also needs to do real writing. It is more important for the child to write a letter to a relative than it is to write a one-line note on a greeting card. Encourage your child to write to relatives and friends. Perhaps your child would enjoy corresponding with a pen pal.

Tips for Parents: Help Your Child to Write Well *(cont.)*

How You Can Help *(cont.)*

4. **Suggest note-taking.** Encourage your child to take notes on trips or outings and to describe what he or she saw. This could include a description of nature walks, a boat ride, a car trip, or other events that lend themselves to note-taking.

5. **Brainstorm.** Talk with your child as much as possible about his/her impressions, and encourage your child to describe people and events to you. If your child's description is especially accurate and colorful, say so.

6. **Write together.** Have your child help you with letters, even such routine ones as ordering items from an advertisement or writing to a business firm. This helps your child to see firsthand that writing is important and truly useful.

7. **Use games.** There are numerous games and puzzles that help a child to increase vocabulary and make a child more fluent in speaking and writing. Remember that building a vocabulary builds confidence. Try crossword puzzles, word games, anagrams, and cryptograms designed especially for children. Flash cards are good, too, and they are easy to make at home.

8. **Suggest making lists.** Most children like to make lists just as they like to count. Making lists is good practice and helps a child to become more organized. Boys and girls might make lists of their records, tapes, baseball cards, dolls, furniture in a room, etc. They could include items they want. It is also good practice to make lists of things to do, schoolwork, dates for tests, social events, and other reminders.

9. **Encourage copying.** If a child likes a particular song, suggest learning the words by writing them down—replaying the song on your CD player or jotting down the words whenever the song is played on a radio program. Also encourage copying favorite poems or quotations from books and plays. Overall, if you show a positive and interested attitude toward writing, your child will, too.

I liked the beach.

The sand was hot.

Tips for Parents: Help Your Child with Math

It is highly likely that when you studied math, you were expected to complete lots of problems accurately and quickly. There was only one way to arrive at your answers, and it was believed that the best way to improve math ability was to do more problems and to do them fast. Today, the focus is less on the quantity of memorized problems and more on understanding the concepts and applying thinking skills to arrive at an answer. While accuracy is always important, a wrong answer may help you and your child discover what your child may not understand. You might find some of the following thoughts helpful when thinking about wrong answers.

- **Realize problems can be solved in different ways.** While problems in math may have only one solution, there may be many ways to get the right answer. When working on math problems with your child, ask, "Could you tell me how you got that answer?" Your child's way might be different from yours. If the answer is correct and the strategy or way of solving it has worked, it is a great alternative. By encouraging children to talk about what they are thinking, we help them to become stronger mathematicians and independent thinkers.

- **Realize doing math in your head is important.** Have you ever noticed that today very few people take their pencil and paper out to solve problems in the grocery, fast food, or department store or in the office? Instead, most people estimate in their heads. Calculators and computers demand that people put in the correct information and that they know if the answers are reasonable. Usually, people look at the answer to determine if it makes sense, applying the math in their heads to the problem. This is the reason why doing math in their heads is so important to our children as they enter the 21st century.

How You Can Help

1. **Help your child do mental math with lots of small numbers in their heads until they develop quick and accurate responses.** Questions such as, "If I have 4 cups, and I need 7 cups, how many more do I need?" or "If I need 12 drinks for the class, how many packages of 3 drinks will I need to buy?"

2. **Encourage your child to estimate the answer.** When estimating, try to use numbers to make it easy to solve problems quickly in your head to determine a reasonable answer. For example, when figuring 18 plus 29, an easy way to get a "close" answer is to think about 20 + 30 = [?].

Tips for Parents: Help Your Child with Math *(cont.)*

How You Can Help *(cont.)*

3. **Allow your child to use strategies that make sense to him or her.** Ask often, "Is your answer reasonable? Is it reasonable that you added 17 and 35 and got 367? Why? Why not?"

4. **Ask your child to explain how the problem was solved.** The response might help you discover if your child needs help with the procedures, the number facts, or the concepts involved. Sometimes the wrong answer to a problem might be because the child thinks the problem is asking another question. For example, when children see the problem $4 + \_ = 9$, they often respond with an answer of 13. They think the problem is asking "What is $4 + 9$?" instead of "4 plus what missing number amount equals 9?"

   You may have learned something your child's teacher might find helpful. A short note or call will alert the teacher to possible ways of helping your child.

5. **Help your child be a risk taker.** Help him or her see the value of examining a wrong answer, and assure him or her that the right answers will come with proper understanding.

6. **Emphasize that math is enjoyable and practical.** Math is part of the everyday world. Even when you are at a fast-food restaurant, point to the prices on the menu and say, "Look! More numbers—they are everywhere!"

Above all, be patient. All children want to succeed. They do not want red marks or incorrect answers. They want to be proud and to make you and the teacher proud. So, the wrong answer tells you to look further, to ask questions, and to see what the wrong answer is saying about the child's understanding.

$$4 + 3 = 7$$

$$2 + 3 = 5$$

$$\begin{array}{r} 9 \\ +\ 1 \\ \hline 10 \end{array}$$

$$\begin{array}{r} 8 \\ +\ 0 \\ \hline 8 \end{array}$$

$$\begin{array}{r} 7 \\ +\ 5 \\ \hline 12 \end{array}$$

$$6 + 3 = 9$$

Tips for Parents: Help Your Child with Reading

You are your child's first teacher. According to the National Institute of Education, the most important thing you can do to help your child succeed in school is to read aloud to him or her. Reading to your child makes him or her feel respected and part of your world. It builds self-esteem.

Reading aloud to your child stimulates the mind, strengthens the imagination, and makes your child curious about the world. Reading aloud will help him or her to understand words, master language, and enable him or her to arrive at school feeling confident.

How You Can Help

1. **Make the reading time special.** Turn off the TV, radio, or anything that will distract from your time together. Story time can be a special part of every day—before bedtime or after a nap. Be responsive at other times, too, if your child brings a book and needs quiet time with you.

2. **Patience!** Reading to children takes time, but you will be letting them know how important they are to you. Children also love to read favorite books over and over again. Being comfortable with a book gives them confidence.

3. **Have your child choose the book you will be reading together.** Sit close together. Hold the book so your child can see it and let him or her turn the pages.

4. **Take time to look at the pictures and talk about them.** Ask your child what he or she thinks is happening or what the characters are feeling.

5. **Make the story come to life by reading with expression.** Change your voice to become different characters or to fit different situations (deep/low, quiet/soft). Ask your child to make special sounds with you—a growling animal or a howling wind.

6. **Stop at interesting points in the story and ask questions** such as "What do you think will happen next?" or "What would you do if you were there?" Help your child relate the story to his or her own experiences by asking questions like "Have you ever felt that way?" Listening to what your child has to say lets him or her know that his or her thoughts are important to you.

7. **Have fun with books and language.** Play games, sing songs, and create rhymes with your child. Read books that offer funny situations and characters so you can enjoy them and laugh together.

8. **Finally, the library can be a familiar and special place for you and your child.** Obtain a library card in your child's name. This will build self-esteem and give him or her a sense of involvement.